D1384759

HELPING UNMARRIED MOTHERS

About the Author

Rose Bernstein, who lives in Brookline, Massachusetts, holds a Bachelor of Arts degree, Cornell University, a Master of Science degree in education, City College of New York, and an M.S.S.W. degree, School of Applied Social Sciences, Western Reserve University. She is a social worker, Information and Referral Service, United Community Services, Boston. She has previously been a supervisor, director of casework (maternity home), researcher and consultant, United States Children's Bureau, and has worked with child guidance clinics, the Red Cross, and various community planning agencies. Mrs. Bernstein is co-author of *Health Services for Unmarried Mothers,* with Elizabeth Herzog, and has had numerous articles and papers published in professional journals.

HELPING

UNMARRIED MOTHERS

Rose Bernstein

ASSOCIATION PRESS, NEW YORK

CONTENTS

5

PREFACE

This book is concerned with two facets of services to unmarried mothers. One has to do with the potential psychological and social hazards of having a child out of wedlock. The other pertains to factors that determine whether an unmarried mother will receive certain services.

One of the principal concerns expressed by many practitioners has been that the unmarried mother who comes to an agency for help frequently does not agree with the helping person about the nature of her difficulty or the kind of help she should have. Practitioners are concerned that an unmarried mother may suffer damaging aftereffects if she does not resolve emotional conflicts that have been stirred up by, or in some instances that have contributed to, the out-of-wedlock pregnancy. Yet efforts to give her such help often come to naught. Most unmarried mothers go to an agency for specific, usually practical, services. Few take kindly to the idea of help with psychological problems. The vast majority withdraw from contact when a plan for the baby has been concluded. As a result, an agency may go to great lengths to get an unmarried mother to accept help it thinks she ought to have, only to find in the end that there is little to show for the effort.

As a staff member in a maternity home, I observed that many unmarried mothers who seemed averse to discussing psychological problems on other occasions were more responsive when seen at points of crisis. At the same time, it also became clear that crisis episodes often involved an unmarried mother's perceptions of herself as a woman and as a mother. On the basis of these observations I developed an approach to the psychological treatment of unmarried mothers that focused on crisis episodes and the maternal role as they emerged in the experiences through which a girl or woman goes as an unmarried mother. This book is in part an elaboration of this approach.

Originally, this individual-oriented approach was to have been the principal focus. However, in applying it at various points of the agency's contact with the unmarried mother, it became evident that individual treatment could not be isolated from more general concerns and that agency policies, community attitudes, and social conditions were likely to have a bearing on what constitutes a crisis for a given unmarried mother and what help she is likely to receive in coping with stress.

The scope of the book has therefore been enlarged to include issues that impinge on individual services. Among them are: eligibility requirements and policies of exclusion; a priori commitments as prerequisites for care; the relevance of agency stipulations to client need; the dichotomizing of services according to the "unholy three"—the plan for the baby, color, and access to services; in short, the question of how it is that whether an agency intends it so or not, the net result of its policies and practices may be that the unmarried mother who most needs its services is least likely to receive them.

Although the orientation is predominantly to social work practice, much of the material may well have implications for practitioners from other disciplines who are called upon to help unmarried mothers plan for themselves and their babies. Moreover, many of the cases indicate how important it is that there be close co-ordination among the several kinds of practitioners who sometimes become involved in the problems of one unmarried mother. From the point of view of effective planning of community services, a multidisciplinary approach is indispensable.

This book is limited, as is any writing, by the point of view of the writer. I hope that the biases arising from my commitment to crisis intervention and the maternal role have been tempered by the judgments of others.

The book is also limited by the nature of the illustrative cases.

With the exception of that of one public child welfare agency, case material was available to me only from maternity homes and voluntary child welfare agencies. These agencies serve approximately one-sixth of all unmarried mothers, the vast majority of whom are middle-class whites who usually surrender their babies for adoption. It is regrettable that this division, which characterizes so much of the health, education, and welfare scene in this country, should be echoed here.

Yet unmarried mothers' problems often transcend class and color and the plan for the baby. Almost any unmarried mother, regardless of her background, is likely to face questions about her relationship with her parents, the involvement of the baby's father, her competence as a mother, and decisions about her own and her baby's future. Many of these questions can generate stresses with which she may need help. It is hoped that some of the treatment principles discussed here can be applied to unmarried mothers in a variety of settings.

In these days of ferment and turmoil, when the urgency of massive social and economic problems is so pressing, one feels almost like apologizing for concentrating on the fine points of individual treatment. To many it may seem like fiddling while Rome burns. Admittedly, problems that arise out of poverty cannot be solved in the interviewing room. No one can imagine that simply taking care of individual situations will provide solutions to problems that require social change and long-range policy planning on a community or national level. Yet it is often in the individual's problems that the broader need becomes manifest. Moreover, one cannot minimize personal pain, whether it has developed out of a sick environment or from internal disequilibrium, if indeed these can be considered separately.

Those charged with the alleviation of suffering must treat it where they find it, whether among the poor or not poor, among black or white. The effort to ease pain often requires skilled service. For no matter how abundant or accessible resources may be, their effectiveness is ultimately determined by the skill and sensitivity with which they are administered in the face-to-face encounter between helper and client. From that point of view, there is room for attention to both individual treatment and the broader problems of community planning and national policy.

The use of crisis and the maternal role in the psychological treatment of unmarried mothers was first developed at Crittenton Hastings House, a maternity home in Boston. I should like to express my gratitude to Mrs. Lilian Bye,* former director, for her support in what was then an unorthodox approach in the treatment of unmarried mothers; to Mrs. Janice Montague, staff member at the maternity home, for her invaluable help in developing this approach; and to the then Board of Trustees of Crittenton Hastings House for permission to use material from the unpublished study, "One Hundred Unmarried Mothers and Their Problems."

I wish also to thank the Child Welfare League of America and the National Association of Social Workers for permission to use portions of my writings that originally appeared in *Child Welfare* and *Social Work*. I am grateful to Mrs. Roberta Hodges for her intelligent and conscientious typing of the manuscript.

My special thanks go to Elizabeth Herzog for an enlightening experience at the United States Children's Bureau, and for the discussions thereafter, which find their echo at many points in the following pages.

To practitioners who shared their experiences and thoughts with me, and to the agencies that provided case material, a massive "Thank you." I am particularly indebted to the participants in workshops and institutes whose comments and questions—supportive, challenging, even on occasion embarrassing, but always stimulating—led me to clarify or otherwise to modify aspects of my thinking.

R. B.

* Mrs. Bye is currently Direktor of The Sozialskolen, Trondheim, Norway.

INTRODUCTION

Nonmarital sex has become increasingly audible and visible in our time; in some quarters marriage seems to be losing its importance as the social framework for sex and childbearing. Perhaps we are approaching a time when unmarried motherhood will be less problem-laden for most women than it is today. It is too soon to know at present. One cannot predict what the attitude toward having an out-of-wedlock child is likely to be in a society that is worried about overpopulation; in which liberation movements press for greater sexual, social, and economic status for women than can be achieved in the kitchen, bedroom, or nursery alone; and in which motherhood for its own sake seems to be losing some of its glamour. Whatever the outlook for unmarried mothers may be in the future, having an out-of-wedlock child today remains for many women an unhappy experience socially and emotionally.

A nonmarital pregnancy can set in motion a series of critical reactions in others that may require drastic changes in the day-to-day living arrangements of the pregnant girl or woman. During the months she is waiting for her baby to be born, and until she concludes a plan for him, she may have to live by rules that negate many of the concepts that are normally considered important in the governing of one's life. Her identity as a prospective mother, as a mother, and as a woman is in dubious status.

The young girl growing up in our society is oriented primarily toward the adult role of wife and mother. Whatever additional career ambitions she may have, and with due regard for militant

11

feminism, her ultimate goal in most instances is to marry and, if possible, to have children.

On becoming pregnant, particularly if it is a first pregnancy, a married woman usually evokes a variety of benign responses from friends and family—admiration, social approval, and perhaps a bit of envy from the less fortunate ones. There are coy jokes about her unpredictable food idiosyncrasies, and her irrational apprehensions are viewed with indulgent tolerance. The first evidences of quickening will occasion excitement, or at least interested discussion. Even if conception was accidental and unwanted, in most instances the married woman eventually relates positively to the coming baby, and her initial unhappiness about being pregnant is forgotten. She will not be called upon to explain why she became pregnant. She will not be asked to understand the symbolic purpose of her sexual relationship with the baby's father, or to identify the emotional conflicts she was trying to resolve via the pregnancy. She does not worry about when "it" will begin to show. She does not need to contrive explanations for a spreading waistline, or to make up reasons for leaving school or work. When she does leave, more likely than not she will depart rich with the spoils of a baby shower.

After she delivers, she will be expected to love her baby and to express her affection in appropriate, identifiable behavior. If, following delivery, she is slow to feel or express the expected maternal feelings for her baby (the not unusual "maternal lag" of newly delivered mothers), she will be encouraged and helped to do so. She will not have to debate whether to keep her baby or to relinquish him for adoption, whether to see him at the hospital, whether to see him just once, or whether to have him regularly for feedings.

When motherhood occurs outside of marriage, however, it loses much of its ordinarily accepted meaning. Having transgressed the unspoken rule that one's sex life is one's private affair as long as one does not make it a matter of public concern by conceiving a child out of wedlock, the unmarried woman experiences motherhood in an atmosphere of social disapproval. She has learned from the mass media and from the professional literature (more widely read by the lay person than is perhaps realized) that her pregnancy is not for real, that it is the symbolic result of underlying emotional problems that she should have dealt with more constructively than through an illicit pregnancy.

In most instances the pregnancy changes her physical and emotional relationship with the baby's father. Often it marks the beginning of the end of their association. If he does express interest initially, his concern is likely to become progressively attenuated with the passing of time. Ultimately she delivers her baby minus the emotional support of the man with whom she had joined in creating this new life, support that is considered so important for the married woman at delivery.

Her relationship with the baby's father is likely to be seen by others primarily in its symbolic, psychological usefulness to her and in terms of its weaknesses. The strengths in him and in their relationship are frequently lost sight of. Needs that often underlie the "normal" impulse to seek out a companion for marriage—a wish to be loved and wanted, fear of loneliness, the need for sexual gratification—are seen as unhealthy when they are associated with an out-of-wedlock pregnancy, and they become matters for speculation and special interpretation.

This downgrading of the unmarried mother's relationship with the baby's father often extends itself to her relationship with her child. Her feelings toward the baby are often suspect. In many ways, both subtle and direct, she becomes aware that as far as her status as a mother is concerned, she is in something of a vacuum. She has to unlearn much of what she had previously perceived as the maternal role and must now accommodate herself to a different concept—that of the nonmother.

If the unmarried mother is white and not poor, she will be expected to surrender her baby for adoption, and much of the time this is what she will do. She will apply to a social agency for the adoption placement of her child, at which time she may be asked to agree to surrender him to the agency directly from the hospital. Thus, contrary to the usual admonitions that one should try to avoid making major decisions at a time of strong emotional distress, she is required to commit herself to a decision of far-reaching proportions when she is likely to be in a state of crisis.

If she needs sheltered living, she may, if she wishes, enter a maternity home. There she is likely to have at her disposal a range of services—casework, group work, group therapy, psychiatric consultation and treatment, pastoral counseling, psychological testing, vocational counseling, health care, and the like. Counseling will also be offered to her parents, to the baby's father, and to his parents. She may find, in fact, that she is living in something akin to a small psychiatric center to which psychiatric trainees come for practice.

In some maternity homes, she will be expected to make "constructive" use of their psychological services. She may be required to attend scheduled therapy or counseling sessions during which she will be expected to respond to questions about her relationship with her parents and with the baby's father and about other intimate matters about which one does not ordinarily expect to be questioned by strangers.

If she is legally and financially independent, she may go to another state to have her baby, preferably one that does not record or report birth status and that permits her to surrender her child for adoption through nonagency channels. In return for living and medical expenses, she can have her baby in anonymity and arrange for his adoption through a private physician or attorney. Her guilt about having borne and given up her illegitimate child may be assuaged by the assurance that he will be raised in a good home with two parents and that she is bringing joy to a childless home.

Following the relinquishment of her child, she will, in most instances, terminate contact with the people from whom she received care. For all practical purposes, she has divested herself of the outward evidences of unmarried motherhood and is now ready to resume her place in the community, to deal with the psychological sequelae of her experiences as best she can.

If the unmarried mother is not white (which more than ninetenths of the time means she is probably Negro), the reasons for her pregnancy are likely to be given a sociological rather than a psychological turn. Her pregnancy is likely to be interpreted in terms of poverty, undereducation, disrupted family life, discrimination, and many of the other ills that beset minorities— and no nonsense about psychological motivations. She will also learn that with an acute shortage of Negro adoptive homes, she has no choice but to keep her baby.

The black unmarried mother will hear references to the influence of cultural factors in Negro illegitimacy. She will be told, contrary to what she hears about white girls, that the Negro suffers neither shame nor social penalty in unmarried motherhood, and that no stigma attaches to the black child born out of wedlock. She will realize that, corresponding to these societal rationalizations, she has little or no access to resources and services that are urged on her white counterpart.*

When she returns to the community with her baby following delivery, she may have to undertake to fulfill the maternal role under social and economic conditions that make it all but impossible for her to meet society's perceptions of what a caring mother should be. She may find that many sources of housing are closed to her, and she often has to make do with inferior living arrangements at exorbitant cost. If she wants to work to support herself and the baby, she finds that suitable day-care services are in short supply or beyond her reach financially, and she may settle for makeshift, often dangerous, arrangements for the care of her child. As an alternative, she may seek support from the Aid to Families with Dependent Children (AFDC) program.

Before she can qualify for assistance she may have to identify and file a complaint against the baby's father, a gesture that at best may be fruitless and humiliating; at worst, actually harmful. If she does receive a grant, it will be small enough to guarantee that she will live in perpetual and inescapable poverty with her child.

She will find, amid cries of "subsidizing illegitimacy," that

* Recently developing comprehensive care programs are a small step toward providing better services to this group.

her behavior has become a matter of public scrutiny. Concepts of a "fit mother" and a "suitable home" take on special meaning in her case, applying almost exclusively to her sexual behavior, with little regard for the conditions of her living or the welfare of the child. The suspicion of a man in the house, based on little more than the presence of a man's jacket on the door, may be enough to place her grant in jeopardy or to precipitate removal of the child from the home, regardless of the quality of the care she gives him.*

In sum, society sees to it that by action or by implication, a woman who is having a child out of wedlock will come away from the experience with an inferior sense of herself as a mother, whether she keeps her baby or relinquishes him for adoption. This downgrading of the maternal image, can do serious injury to the later maternal functioning of the woman whose perception of herself as a mother is thus impaired. The helping person, as an agent of society, can have an important influence in preventing or reducing such damage. That influence is what this book is about.

* A few states have relaxed some of these and other strictures on eligibility for AFDC. However, the general situation across the country remains essentially unaltered. If anything, there is a push toward greater restrictions, as evidenced in the 1967 "freeze" legislation and in the more euphemistically phrased 1969 "workfare" proposals.

1

PREGNANCY, MATERNITY, AND CRISIS

Crisis intervention with unmarried mothers is based on the assumption that out-of-wedlock pregnancy constitutes an extended emotional and social crisis that results when the biologic and psychologic stresses of pregnancy are intensified by the social stresses of the out-of-wedlock status. The experience contains potentials for growth or damage, particularly in connection with the unmarried mother's perception of herself as a mother and as a woman. This theory holds that intervention should address itself to critical episodes, with emphasis on major decisions and maternal role.[1]

Pregnancy itself, even in marriage, is increasingly being interpreted as a potentially critical experience. Caplan suggests:

. . . pregnancy is to be regarded as a period of increased susceptibility to crisis. Factors operating on the biological plane in the expectant mother interact reciprocally with factors in her physiological functioning and in the interpersonal relationships of her family group. . . . Pregnancy may impose characteristic stress on each of these planes and in many cases leads to disequilibrium in the general system and sub-systems.[2]

Crisis usually requires major changes in a person's customary ways of living and being. As a result, it can disrupt current functioning and render ineffective previously workable ways of dealing with life situations. It can distort a person's customary mode of reaction, expose latent vulnerabilities, and revive unresolved or partially resolved problems from the past that may heretofore have been manageable. Rapoport notes: "It has been observed by various investigators that during a crisis memories of old problems which are linked symbolically to the present are stimulated and may emerge into consciousness. . . ." [3] And Caplan reports that "a usual finding [in connection with a pregnant woman] is a revival of memories of conflict with her mother during childhood, memories of early sibling rivalry, memories of conflicts and guilt over masturbation during adolescence, and so on." [4]

With the revival of old problems and a breakdown in the customary way of managing his affairs, a person is inclined to reassess his former ways of meeting life's tasks and to look for better ways. He is more susceptible to change and to the intervention of others than he would be in less troubled times. It is as though the psychological system were trying to compensate for the trouble that has been stirred up by laying the basis for a corrective experience. In other words, a person in crisis is often a person who can be helped.

. . . old problems . . . can be uncovered and dealt with by relatively brief therapeutic intervention. . . . The crisis with its mobilization of energy operates as a "second chance" in correcting earlier faulty problem-solving. . . . A little help, rationally directed and purposefully focused at a strategic time is more effective than more extensive help given at a period of less emotional accessibility.[5]

Caplan finds a marked susceptibility to help with psychological discomforts during pregnancy:

If a patient is given any encouragement she will talk about these old matters with more and more urgency as pregnancy progresses. . . . The special importance of the revival of these problems from the preventive psychiatry point of view is that their re-emergence provides a possibility of a better solution than was achieved in the past, with a resultant increase in the woman's maturity.[6]

The Crisis Compounded

The primary crisis for an unmarried mother starts when she first realizes she is pregnant. It extends for an undetermined time after the birth of the baby, depending upon the extent to which subsequent events perpetuate or reactivate residuals from the pregnancy and from the immediate postpartal period.

The primary crisis is punctuated by a series of subcrises that may be precipitated by changes in a woman's biological, physical, social, or interpersonal circumstances. A subcrisis may be triggered by developments in the fetus (for example, the first sensation of life, "engagement"), by changes in the expectant mother's health, by events that threaten her school or job status, by changes in attitude on the part of her parents or the baby's father, by having to apply to a community agency for help, or by a host of decisions she has to make, not the least of which has to do with the birth of the baby and plans for his future. The precipitating event itself may not be of great moment, but it triggers a crisis because it exposes a condition or poses a task that the woman feels incapable of handling. Often it is a condition or task that underscores the fact that she is having a baby out of wedlock.

Whatever the triggering event, the point at which a woman feels unable to cope with her circumstances is the point at which she is likely to show symptoms of crisis. Symptoms can take many forms. Unmarried mothers seen at points of crisis exhibit a whole range of reactions—denial, hostility, suspicion, excessive guilt, insufficient guilt, depression, an absence of observable affect, and even, on occasion, inappropriate euphoria. Generalized feelings of inadequacy and failure are not uncommon at such times. Many women give a history of deprivation in primary relationships, with chronic feelings of having been unloved and unwanted. These reactions, compounded of past and current stresses, may be appropriate responses to a threatening situation, or they may denote underlying emotional pathology. In any event, they are signals of distress and may indicate a need for psychological help.

Help should be available as close as possible to the precipitating event and should address itself to those aspects of the event that the client finds most distressing. Ideally it would be good if help could be patterned after the crisis episodes themselves—that is, concentrated in a series of closely clustered interviews at the time of the acute stress.

Following this contact there may be a period of relative tranquility during which contact can be minimal. During such periods the client can consolidate the understandings she has gained during the time of concentrated help, testing herself as she applies them to other aspects of her situation and assesses her ability to cope with later events.

It is in a sense an ad hoc, operational approach. Each episode becomes a major subunit of intervention that, though related to preceding and subsequent episodes, as well as to the over-all treatment objectives, is geared to short-term goals that can be achieved in a relatively brief time. Sometimes a rapid succession of three or four half-hour interviews at a time of intense anxiety and heightened receptivity can be more effective than a whole series of prescheduled hour-long interviews at weekly intervals. At other times one or two extended sessions may be indicated.

The disadvantage of the planned appointment is that often a crisis has passed its peak by the time a client arrives for the interview. Having somehow managed to weather the worst of it, she may feel there is nothing to be gained by warming over the turmoil through which she has just passed, and an opportunity to help her is lost. This approach does not rule out planned appointments, but rather makes room for other patterns of help.

Admittedly, allowing for clustered contacts tailored to crisis episodes can present formidable administrative problems for an agency. Moreover, since this aspect of crisis intervention was worked out in a maternity home, it would no doubt have to be modified in order to apply in other settings.

Unmarried mothers, like other people in trouble, do not always accept psychological help when they need it. They can resist crisis intervention as vigorously as they can any other approach. If an unmarried mother refuses help at a time of acute stress, it often means she is unable or unwilling to face it at the time it occurs. If, as a result, the crisis remains largely unresolved, she remains in a psychological state of crisis readiness after the critical event itself has passed. Mounting tensions from the unresolved crisis may make her irritable and hyperactive, vulnerable to slight happenings. If the supports that have been bolstering her defenses weaken, and the inner pressures can no longer be contained, the unresolved crisis is likely to erupt in connection with a subsequent event that is linked to the earlier one. When this happens, critical elements from both episodes overlap, interact, and reinforce one another. Neither the present crisis nor the earlier one can be resolved independently of the other. In a sense the later crisis offers a woman a new opportunity—a "second chance," so to speak—to deal with a task she was unable to face when it first emerged.

A "Second Chance"

Dorothy K.'s experience indicates how an unmarried pregnant woman who at first rejected the thought that she had been abandoned by the baby's father was subsequently able to come to grips with it in connection with an episode that involved her burgeoning feelings for the coming baby.

Dorothy K., aged twenty-eight, applied to an adoption agency when she was four months pregnant. She had given up her secretarial job, had sublet her apartment in another city, and was now working as a mother's helper with a local family. She found the people congenial and tactful, and enjoyed her work.

She was to enter a maternity home about six weeks prior to her expected date of confinement. In the meantime, she was to attend the home's prenatal clinic. She was meticulous about health routines and diet.

Dorothy was restrained, but not unfriendly, with the worker. She talked mostly about practical matters, refusing from the first to talk about the baby's father. She angrily rejected the worker's suggestion that she, the worker, see him for preplacement family history, and became visibly agitated when an effort was made to pursue the matter. When, after several weeks, the worker commented that Dorothy had scarcely mentioned the baby and that she seemed to be avoiding talking about him, Dorothy replied that there was not much to talk about. She hoped the baby would be healthy, and she was following the doctor's orders to make sure there would be no trouble. She said she had everything worked out. She was planning not to see the baby after it was born and hoped the agency would permit her to sign an early relinquishment. She did not see what else there was to talk about. To the worker's comment that many unmarried expectant mothers find their feelings changing later in the pregnancy, and that often these feelings are troublesome, Dorothy insisted no such thing would happen to her.

In the following weeks Dorothy became more and more tense, and repeatedly asked for delays in her admission to the maternity home. She felt fine and could see no reason for not remaining in her present home. She gave as her main reason for not wanting to move the excuse that she hated the idea of living with "a bunch of pregnant teenagers." The worker said she did not think the maternity home would want to take medical responsibility for Dorothy if she was not in residence, but offered to make inquiries for her.[7]

Seven weeks before her baby was due Dorothy began to show signs of delivering prematurely. After a week's stay in the hospital, it was considered safe for her to leave, provided she could have close supervision and plenty of rest. She had no choice but to enter the maternity home for the remainder of her pregnancy.

When the worker visited her at the home two days after she had been admitted, Dorothy greeted her with an outburst that had more of panic than of anger in it. She couldn't stand living with a bunch of pregnant kids who didn't know what it was all about. She hated being surrounded by people all the time, having to go to chapel, being told what to eat, and so forth.

No, she guessed maybe the rules weren't as rigid as she had made them out to be. Yes, she could stay away from chapel if she wished, and there were plenty of opportunities to be by herself when she felt like it. She admitted that it was not the home itself that was so hard to take, but what it stood for.

Dorothy spoke of the feeling of terror that overcame her when she walked into the maternity home and realized that her baby was going to be illegitimate, after all. She couldn't stand the sight of herself pregnant, and she couldn't stand the sight of all those pregnant girls and women. She must have been out of her mind before, living in a dream world, hoping the thing inside her would stay there forever and never become a live baby. And she had foolishly clung to the notion that eventually Andy, the baby's father, would come and take her away from this dismal mess.

When Dorothy first realized she had been abandoned by the baby's father, she could not tolerate the thought. She rejected it before it had a chance to take shape, and retreated into a fantasy about his someday coming to claim her. As long as her living arrangement supported this self-deception, she was able to avoid facing the facts.

As the pregnancy progressed, feelings about the coming baby, increasingly difficult to deny, became linked with her feelings about the baby's father. They converged in the crisis that was precipitated by her admission to the maternity home. In association with other girls who were also pregnant and unmarried, she could no longer avoid facing the fact that the baby's father was not going to marry her and that her baby was going to be born out of wedlock. Her earliest fantasy of the perpetual, never-to-be-born fetus—the nonbaby, so to speak—and of rescue by the baby's father was no longer useful. She had no choice but to face the realities she had until then been trying so hard to deny. Having faced those realities, Dorothy began to relive some of the feelings she had been unable to face when she first suspected she could not count on Andy.

In two subsequent interviews Dorothy talked about the parallels between her feelings about the baby and her reaction when the full impact of Andy's indifference had struck her. She could not believe that her two years' association with him, which had meant so much to her and which she thought had meant a great deal to him also, had suddenly become so meaningless. She was afraid the same thing would happen with the baby; she would love it and would then have to lose it, as she knew she must. Rather than have to go through that experience, she tried not to think of the baby at all.

But as time passed and she felt the baby moving inside her, she could not stop thinking about it. Sometimes she could almost feel herself holding it in her arms. This frightened her. Uppermost in her mind was the fear that her resolve not to see the baby after it was born would not hold up and that this breakdown in her controls would destroy all her previous efforts to keep her thoughts and feelings contained.

There is no telling what the breaking points are likely to be for an individual unmarried mother or which of a number of critical episodes she will be unable to cope with. One woman may take in stride an event that another may find all but disabling. By the same token, an event may vary in its impact on a woman, depending upon when it happens. What might be a shattering misfortune this week may be little more than a bearable disappointment three weeks later. Much depends upon the woman's physical condition at the time, her stage of pregnancy, her external circumstances, the inner strengths and vulnerabilities the event has touched off, and probably a number of other influences.

The helping person needs to be ready to intervene at whatever point an unmarried mother is ready to accept help, which sometimes may not be until after the baby is born. But it is never too late when recurrent crises are involved. Even the few days between the birth of the baby and the mother's discharge from the hospital can be used effectively. In fact, the sense of urgency that comes when there is little time to deal with an acute problem can motivate an unmarried mother to make optimum use of the time she does have left.

Decisions and Crisis

The crises Dorothy K. went through were rooted in identifiable conditions—her abandonment by the baby's father and her burgeoning feelings for her baby. Sometimes a crisis results not so much from a specific condition or event, but rather because an important decision has to be made. When the stakes are high, when the decision is likely to have far-reaching consequences, and when it allows no margin for error, one is likely to be cautious about committing oneself.

The decisions unmarried mothers have to make are among the difficult ones. These decisions have to be made under conditions of restricted maneuverability and abnormal pressures—pressures of time and emotion that do not allow for testing, exploring, and other procedures that are ordinarily considered essential to sound decision-making. The threat of loss may be great no matter what a woman decides. Unable to make up her mind, she may wind up in a panic of indecision.

She is in fact at a point of crisis, in need of help and often ready to accept it. She needs to break through the impasse, to separate out the major choices, to assess what is to be gained or lost from each, and to come to a conclusion about what she wants to do. She needs to identify factors that are keeping her from making a decision or from acting on it, and she needs to understand what she must do in order to clear away the obstacles to action.

The quest for answers to her immediate difficulty often reveals the existence of a chronic problem. When an unmarried mother comes to a standstill in connection with an important decision, it may well be that an unresolved conflict from the past has become linked with elements in the current crisis, thus thwarting her efforts to solve it. If the current crisis is to be resolved, the chronic problem will also have to be dealt with. This was Lori L.'s problem.

Lori, aged twenty-two, applied for maternity home care when she was three months pregnant. She was to start prenatal care as an outpatient, the date for her admission to be decided later. She was from another city, living away from home.

In the second of two exploratory interviews with the social worker (to get acquainted with the home and to discuss the role of the social worker, plans for the baby, the kind of help Lori thought she would need, and so forth), the worker remarked on how tentative Lori's responses were, as though she were not sure she was in the right place.

Lori agreed this was so. She was not sure she was doing the right thing; in fact, she was not sure she really knew what she was doing at all. Coming to the maternity home was her parents' idea. It was their way of trying to keep her from marrying Mike, the baby's

father, although they said it was because they thought she would
see things more clearly away from home. They had not been enthu-
siastic about her relationship with Mike in the first place. They
disapproved of a "forced" marriage, particularly since they would
then have to make explanations about their "premature" grandchild.

Lori and Mike had known each other for over a year. They were
in love and had assumed they would someday marry. In fact, they
had begun to talk about dates, and Lori was confident that her
parents would not oppose the marriage once they were convinced
that she and Mike were serious about it. When Lori became pregnant, they decided not to delay. Now she did not know what to do.
She wanted to marry Mike, but she did not want to hurt her parents.
She was no nearer a solution at this time than she was six weeks
before, and she just kept going around in circles.

Mike had been patient, but she could not expect him to wait
forever. She would not blame him if he got tired of her dilly-dallying
and called the whole thing off.

Lori knew what she wanted to do, but she could not act on
her choice because it brought her in conflict with her parents.
Yet she had withstood their opposition before she became pregnant in connection with the same decision; namely, to marry
Mike. Why, then, was it so much more difficult for her to handle
the same question now?

The indications were that her being pregnant out of wedlock
made the difference. It precipitated a crisis that stirred up old
problems in her relationship with her parents, and she became
immobilized as she contemplated a major step of which they
did not approve. She would probably not be able to get beyond
this impasse unless she could come to grips with some of the
sources of her indecision.

The worker asked whether Lori usually reacted this way when
she and her parents differed about something. Lori said most of the
time she tried to avoid disagreements with them. Obliquely at first,
and then more directly as she went on, she talked about her attempts
during her last two years in high school to free herself from her
parents' controls.

In the next two interviews she reviewed a number of incidents
relating to this problem. Most of the disagreements had to do with

social matters, such as who her friends should be, whether she should go to a particular affair, and whether her escort was suitable. Often she would start by trying to have her way. Sometimes she succeeded. Much of the time she did not. Since her parents always seemed so sure of their position, she figured they must be right. Besides, half the time it did not matter enough to oppose them. Sometimes when she gave in, she would boil inside and have awful thoughts. But usually everything would be all right by the next day.

Did Lori think her parents might be right about Mike now, as she used to think they were about her dates and friends in high school? Yes, sometimes she did feel that way. At least they were right about some things. They must have suspected that she and Mike were having relations. They never questioned her about it, but continually cautioned her about a "mistake," warning her that men rarely marry girls they have fun with. She thinks that is why they dislike him.

The worker pointed out that Lori's parents had objected to Mike before she became pregnant; yet she still planned to marry him. What was different now? Had she detected a difference in Mike's attitude?

Lori said she did not know why, but when she found out she was pregnant, it seemed to spoil everything. Nothing had really changed. And yet suddenly all the little things—in Mike, in herself, in the relationship—became very large, things they had both been aware of all along but that had not seemed to matter until she became pregnant. It was as though the whole relationship had become tainted.

Luckily Mike was the kind of guy with whom you could talk things over. When Lori told him how she felt, they sat down and took inventory of their whole relationship—the good and the bad. It really became funny after a while, and they kiddingly decided to set up an assets and liabilities ledger. If ever she had any doubts about Mike, or about her feelings for him, she did not have them any more. She knew now more than ever that they were for each other.

Having clarified her feelings about Mike and having confirmed her desire to marry him, Lori now had to deal with the obstacles that were standing in the way of her decision. Guilt about her "awful" thoughts had become linked with guilt about her sexual activity and the resultant pregnancy. Her confidence in her own judgment, probably tenuous to begin with, had been shaken in the face of her parents' opposition. Emotionally she was unable to carry out a decision that intellectually she felt to be correct. The ploy she had used as an adolescent—overt submission and covert rebellion—was neither appropriate nor workable in her present circumstances. If Lori was to break through her impasse, she would have to separate her adolescent self as the daughter of her parents from her maturing self as the partner in an adult relationship with an important decision to make.

The worker pointed out that since Lori seemed fairly certain about what she wanted to do, the question now seemed to be whether she could do what she felt was right for herself and Mike without hurting her parents. Did Lori think it would necessarily mean being bad friends with them if she were to decide that the decision concerning marriage was essentially hers and Mike's to make? The worker wondered whether, in fact, it might not put the relationship on a sounder footing if Lori could shed some of the resentments that apparently had been building up over the years because she had been accepting decisions that were not her own.

Lori was not sure she could go against her parents' wishes, but thought it was worth trying. She wondered whether she was up to it, but she had to do something. "This is more important than who should take me to a dance. This is me, Mike, and the baby." Besides, in spite of all her fuming about her parents' interfering in her affairs, she had to admit that they were basically kind and loving. She would like to work this thing out so as not to hurt them.

During the next interview Lori decided to go home to inform her parents of her decision to marry Mike. On her return she came in for a brief final interview. She told the worker that, except for an initial nervousness, the talk with her parents had been more comfortable than she had anticipated. Mike had come with her. He was polite but firm with her parents, and apparently convinced them "their little girl had grown up."

A major factor in the resolution of this crisis was that Lori arrived at her decision through a step-by-step process. In order to make a responsible choice she had to examine the ingredients in her current situation and reassess past events. She had to consider the impact of her decisions on those who, besides herself, would be affected by them. Having weighed the various factors, she had to be ready to take responsibility for the probable consequences of her choice.

The worker did not take sides in the disagreement between Lori and her parents so far as the decision itself was concerned. She did not say that Lori should or should not marry Mike. Rather, on the assumption that as an adult Lori had the right to make her own decision, the focus was on the psychological impediments that had to be cleared away if Lori was to find her own solution. Had Lori acted without going through this process and had accepted a ready-made solution, she would have remained prone to repeated crises to which the unresolved conflict predisposed her.

There are times, of course, when the helping person should state her position on the merits of a proposed solution. If the evidence is unmistakable that the outcome of a given action is likely to be harmful to the unmarried mother or to others, this should be pointed out unequivocally. The trouble is there are so few occasions when the evidence is unmistakable. Much of the time it is difficult to judge the merits of a decision because one does not know, at the time it has to be made, how it is going to turn out. Out-of-wedlock pregnancy is an experience in biological and psychological change. It can bring about some remarkable and unanticipated alterations for good or ill in a woman who has gone through it. Often the effects do not manifest themselves for months. Moreover, one cannot predict how later events may intervene to alter the quality of a decision that was made several months before.

For example, Lori not only made substantial strides in dealing with her problem but also learned a way of dealing with conflict that can stand her in good stead in other life situations. It would be vain, however, to claim that the problem had thus been laid to rest. One cannot predict how enduring her gains will be or how well they equip her for the added tasks of wife and mother. One cannot know whether her parents will allow her to carry out these roles responsibly or whether Mike will be able to satisfy her more-than-usual dependency needs.

In the face of the many unpredictable factors regarding the outcome of decisions unmarried mothers have to make, the decision itself must often take second place to the benefits that can accrue when an unmarried mother is encouraged to make her own decisions, unless, of course, there are clear hazards. Sometimes the mere fact that her right to make a decision has been respected can be a major factor in the way she approaches other aspects of her situation. The woman who is helped to a successful experience in responsible decision-making is likely to emerge from unwed motherhood with increased confidence and an enhanced sense of herself.

Resistance, Self-Determination, Denial

The first thing the unmarried mother is likely to lose is her right to make important decisions. The agency or community tells her what she must do if she is to receive the services she needs. Whether she remains in school or leaves is often decided by others. In most instances the plan for the baby is pre-determined. Often these matters are decided without her being able to state her own preferences.

This denial of her right to make her own decisions may, in her mind, have a distinctly punitive connotation. The implication is that having conceived a child out of wedlock, she has forfeited the right to control significant aspects of her life. She must accept the decisions of others because not to do so would entail risks she is in no position to take.

As a woman in crisis, she is prone to feelings of guilt and self-depreciation. If the attitudes of others, particularly those who act as agents of society, are demeaning to her self-esteem, her own image of herself is likely to be correspondingly depreciated. One of the outstanding hallmarks of a devalued person in our society is the restriction of choices and decision-making.[8]

An unmarried mother's right to self-determination is likely to be risked at two major crisis points in her experience: *a*), when she applies to a community agency for help, and *b*), in connection with her relationship with the baby. The special problems each of these issues presents are discussed in later chapters. In a more general sense, the question usually revolves around her reluctance to accept help with psychological problems when the helping person thinks she should have it. Often the concern is that this resistance indicates she is not facing the realities of her circumstances. It is thought that, insofar as this resistance can reflect an unhealthy psychological status, it can jeopardize her mental health and the welfare of her baby.

It is difficult to know sometimes whether resistance to receiving help denotes pathological denial. Perhaps it is more important to understand what purpose the behavior is serving than to give it a label. Under some circumstances, in fact, denial can be considered normal. For example, many pregnant married women do not relate to the fetus as a living entity until some time into the second trimester, frequently not until the first quickening is felt or until there are visible physical signs. If, in the early months, there are no outward evidences of pregnancy and no nausea or other discomfort, with only the results of a laboratory test or changes in the menstrual cycle to go by, the baby often remains remote and unreal to the prospective mother. Not infrequently married women whose conceptions were unplanned or initially unwanted cling to a feeble hope during this period that perhaps there was an error in diagnosis and that they are not pregnant after all. In view of the complications that attend pregnancy out of wedlock, it is to be expected that the normal denial found in early pregnancy among married women would be accentuated in unmarried women. For them denial may reflect a desperate hope rather than a distortion of reality.

Unless an unmarried mother is seriously disoriented, it is a fairly safe guess that she is not so much denying the substance of her situation as she is trying to avoid facing some of its more threatening implications. Facing reality in her case may mean having to acknowledge that she has been abandoned by the baby's father, that she is in social or economic jeopardy, and that either she will have to relinquish a baby she may love or that she will have to keep a baby she is not sure she is going to love. Her denial attaches itself to those segments of her situation that are momentarily intolerable to her, even while other parts of her behavior bespeak her awareness of the realities.

For example, Dorothy K. tried to deny that she had been abandoned by the baby's father. She avoided any discussion or action that would acknowledge the abandonment. Yet in other ways she showed that she realized she was pregnant and unmarried. She took appropriate steps to protect herself from the social hazards of unwed motherhood and observed the necessary routines to protect the health of her baby and herself. She was able to accommodate herself to the outward demands of her circumstances while preserving for herself a defended island to which she could retreat emotionally when the implications of her circumstances became intolerable to her.

In this sense, temporary denial can have a healing function. If the realities of the moment come to an unmarried mother as a shock, or if she feels unequal to the psychological tasks required of her, warding off a head-on encounter can have a benign effect. At such times denial can serve as a psychic splint, a way of resting a bruised part of the personality and postponing the encounter until she feels better able to cope with the problem.

Intervention that is therapeutically oriented should take into account the need for such psychological protections and should respect an unmarried mother's right to use them. If an unmarried mother has to defend herself against repeated attempts to get her to accept help she does not want, her psychic energies are likely to be diverted from the important task of self-healing which crisis often liberates.

Is Crisis Intervention Enough?

In some instances crisis intervention is little more than a holding action, serving primarily to keep an unmarried mother together psychologically as she goes from one crisis to another. She manages to weather critical episodes, but her decisions are stopgaps rather than solutions. Neither the immediate crises nor the old conflicts they have stirred up are adequately dealt with. When the primary crisis is past and the turmoil is over, she is still in a state of crisis. She can neither come to terms with the events she has just gone through nor accommodate herself to the tasks that lie ahead.

Having a child out of wedlock is merely a last straw, the added strain that cannot be tolerated by a psychological system that is already burdened with severe chronic problems. Crisis intervention is not enough to resolve satisfactorily either the immediate crises or the chronic problem. Treatment has to be directed toward the underlying problem itself. In such a situation, the most recent crisis becomes the point of departure from which the unmarried mother can be helped to accept more extensive psychological help.

Dorothy K. presented such a situation. Following the birth of the baby Dorothy was in a lather of indecision. She could not tolerate not seeing him; yet she was afraid of what would happen to her if she did see him. She was alternately depressed and agitated. In consultation with a psychiatrist (she refused to see him herself), it was decided that Dorothy should be encouraged to see the baby at least once, that it would be better to risk her reaction to seeing him than to expose her to the endless fantasying that her not seeing him could promote.

Dorothy asked to be accompanied by a nurse when she went to the nursery to see the baby the night before he was to go into agency care and she was to leave the hospital. The nurse reported that, on seeing the baby, Dorothy burst into tears and sobbed, "My own child, and I have no feeling for him!"

In a brief interview just before Dorothy was to be discharged, the worker pointed out that in view of the upsetting experiences she had been through, and in view of the adjustment ahead of her, it would be good if Dorothy allowed the worker to help her through this period. At first Dorothy said she would like to try to manage on her own, explaining that she reacted as she did at the hospital because of the drugs she had received during labor. However, when she came in to sign surrender papers two weeks later she asked for an appointment.

Dorothy opened the interview with: "I feel as though I'm going to pieces." She said she had no ambition to look for a job and would not be able to keep her mind on her work even if she did find one. She could not get the baby out of her mind, constantly wondering whether she had been right in seeing him only once.

Her feelings about the baby were so mixed up. She kept telling herself that no matter what happened afterward, the baby was born of a love relationship. Most of the time she did love him, and then she would have a surge of feeling for Andy too. Then suddenly she would feel such hate for Andy that she would start hating the baby. It was love and hate all at once, but it seemed mostly that she could not let go of the hate.

She could see that in some ways she had invited Andy's poor treatment of her. She took too much from him, never stood up to him even when she knew he was wrong. She told herself it was because she loved him, but the real reason for much of her behavior was that she did not want to lose him. "If I lost him, at least I wouldn't be in this trouble now."

No, she was not usually so compliant with others, "except maybe with my father." Dorothy spoke of how, as an only child, she was expected to be both son and daughter to her father. She had no interest in fishing, yet went with her father because he wanted her company. She switched from art to a secretarial course because he insisted art was no career for a woman. She was never sure when he would ask her to do something that he would have wanted a son to do, or when she would have to give up something because he did not think it was appropriate for a woman.

After more discussion in this vein, Dorothy realized that she needed help and accepted referral to a psychiatrist. Six months after referral she was in active treatment.

The separation from the baby precipitated a crisis that climaxed the several preceding ones through which Dorothy had gone. The breakdown in her efforts to pick up the thread of a normal life forced into the open a long-standing problem that she had avoided during other episodes, when her energies were engaged with immediate crises. Her failure to cope with critical tasks in her experience as an unmarried mother—namely, her relationship with the baby and her feelings about the baby's father—crystallized the underlying problem: her confused sense of herself as a woman and the conflict about her relationship with her father.

Crisis Intervention and Social Work

Crisis intervention with unmarried mothers is concerned with helping the pregnant and newly-delivered woman to cope with the crucial tasks she faces as an unmarried mother. It is one of several possible approaches and has its unpredictabilities and its unexpected outcomes, its failures as well as its successes.

However, some attributes of crisis intervention make it particularly appropriate as an instrument of social work help. It focuses on current reality, on social role, and on social functioning,[9] rather than on dynamic etiological factors from the past. As a now-oriented approach that addresses itself to problems of immediate urgency, it is likely to be more readily understood and accepted by the client who has not come for psychological help. Insofar as it focuses on the effects and concomitants of circumstances rather than on causes, it does not lead to an early confrontation with deficiencies in past behavior which can be threatening to someone who is already struggling with questions of self-esteem. Nevertheless, it does not rule out the exploration of underlying problems and in fact can, when indicated, serve as a point of departure for more extensive psychological help, as happened with Dorothy K. Because crisis intervention deals with episodes and aspects of functioning rather than with personality dynamics, it can focus selectively on those portions of the personality that are involved in the acute stress and that are therefore more susceptible of change.

Crisis intervention with unmarried mothers is essentially an empirical approach. It seems to work well in many situations. Yet it needs to be tested and compared with other approaches and with crisis intervention in other problem situations. There is no typology to indicate for whom and under what circumstances it is likely to be most effective. In this, perhaps the unmarried mothers themselves are apt to be the best sources of information and guidance to the helping person.

NOTES

1. For several reports on studies in crisis, see Howard J. Parad, ed., *Crisis Intervention: Selected Readings* (New York: Family Service Association of America, 1965), pp. 75–298.
2. Gerald Caplan, "Psychological Aspects of Maternity Care," *Bulletin of Maternal Welfare* 4 (November–December 1957), p. 1.
3. Lydia Rapoport, "The State of Crisis: Some Theoretical Considerations," in Parad, *Crisis Intervention,* p. 25.
4. Caplan, *op. cit.,* p. 5.
5. Rapoport, *op. cit.,* p. 30.
6. *Ibid.*
7. Some maternity homes have recently changed this policy and give outpatient health and counseling service throughout the pregnancy.
8. For a discussion of client determination and the handling of resistance, see Saul Bernstein, "Self-Determination: King or Citizen in the Realm of Values?", *Social Work* 5 (January 1960), pp. 3–8. For additional articles concerned with self-determination see *Values In Social Work: A Re-examination* (New York: National Association of Social Workers, 1967).
9. Werner W. Boehm, "The Nature of Social Work," *Social Work* 3 (April 1958), pp. 10–18.

2

THE
REQUEST
FOR HELP

When an unmarried mother applies to a community agency for help, she in effect admits that, short of a miscarriage, her chances for avoiding unwed motherhood have all but vanished. She knows she is going to be pregnant for a more or less predictable length of time, at the end of which time her out-of-wedlock baby will be born.

She brings to the agency her personal strengths and vulnerabilities as they interact with the experiences she has had from the time she realized she was pregnant to the present: efforts at marriage or abortion; reactions of family, friends, and the baby's father; advice from pastor, physician, or attorney; and possibly an unsuccessful application to another community agency. She is fairly definite about the kind of help she needs and is likely to see it primarily in practical terms—adoption, financial assistance, schooling, sheltered living, legal aid, and so forth. These are what she has come to the agency for, and these are what she asks for. Usually these are also likely to be the things she needs.

The worker knows, however, that the presenting request is often only part of the story—that a practical need is frequently tied to emotional distress. Sometimes it masks another, more urgent problem. If the applicant has identified the source of her distress incompletely or inaccurately, the service she asks for is likely to be ineffectual and, in some instances, inappropriate.

Identifying the Problem

Therefore, an early task for applicant and agency is to arrive at some perspective on her problem—to identify the urgent stresses, to examine the applicant's solutions as well as other possibilities, and to establish the terms of their ongoing association; in short, to see whether she and the agency can do business with each other.

A first step is to come to an understanding about the nature of the applicant's problem. If it turns out that the solution she proposes is inappropriate to her need, she can be helped to redefine her problem and to look for more appropriate solutions.

Beth R., aged twenty-three, applied for early admission to a maternity home when she was little more than three months pregnant. She was friendly and outwardly poised, but at times seemed on the verge of tears. She loved her work, had a comfortable apartment, and enjoyed good relationships with friends and professional associates.

In response to the worker's comment that it seemed early for Beth to come into residence, particularly since her condition was not noticeable, Beth at first said this would be a convenient time for her to leave work because of a changeover in assignments at her office. If she came into the maternity home she could carry off a story about going home for an extended visit. "Still," I suppose people would wonder if all of a sudden I announced I was going home for six months." She was puzzled about why she was going to all this trouble. Her friends and associates were liberal about these things, and she did not think an out-of-wedlock pregnancy would be frowned on—at least not openly. She guessed, however, since she would be giving the baby up, she might as well "play the game" from the first.

The worker thought it would be possible for Beth to come into residence early, but she could not help wondering whether it really would help. If Beth had too long a stay, she might get bored and impatient. The worker suggested that Beth think a little more about the timing of her admission.

Beth admitted that maybe she had not thought things out too carefully. "I guess I just haven't been thinking, period." Maybe she had better not rush in this way. She had never dreamed she would ever have to come to a place like this. She cried as she said how disappointed she was in the baby's father.

Beth came with a request that was palpably inappropriate to her problem. The worker pointed out some of the incongruities in her plan—the contradiction between the supposedly liberal attitudes of her friends and colleagues on the one hand, and her sense of urgency about going into residence on the other, and the disadvantages in her proposed solution. As Beth reassessed her request, she was able to identify a more compelling source of her distress, namely, a problem in relation to the baby's father.

Beth said she and Tim had planned to marry in about a year. She was shocked that he did not suggest they marry right away when she told him she was pregnant. He thought they should not rush into marriage without thinking it over more carefully; he was not sure they were ready for it.

Was it Beth's impression that Tim had begun to lose interest in her? Sometimes she wondered, but mostly she did not think so, at least judging by his outward behavior. He was as attentive and as solicitous of her now as he had always been, if not more so. He telephoned frequently and visited her as often as the arduous trip would allow. (He was working out of state.)

Maybe he did not realize how hurt she was at his hesitancy. Yet he was usually a sensitive person. Maybe she should have told him how she felt, but she just could not. Every time she tried, she would get so upset that she would have all she could do to keep from crying. She wanted to be sure he was marrying her because he wanted to, not because she was pregnant.

Yes, she guessed she had always been uneasy about Tim's real feelings, more so than she wanted to admit. Always at the back of her mind was the thought that if anything did happen, she would be stuck with the pregnancy and Tim could do what he liked. She must have half expected something like this would happen. It was funny that she had never raised the question with him.

She admitted that perhaps she had jumped the gun in applying to the maternity home so soon. She had done it on an impulse, hoping maybe it would wake him up when he found out about it. But she did not know how Tim felt about it because she had not told him she was applying.

The worker pointed out that although it was understandable that Beth would want to shake Tim up, it was not likely to be a satisfactory way of handling such an important problem. If Beth had to resort to indirection rather than talking things out, it could cause trouble for her whether she married Tim or not.

Beth realized she was not handling things right. She did not know what got into her, acting like such a baby. She could see there would be little point in entering the home until she knew she needed to. She accepted the worker's offer to help her in the meantime to understand why it was so difficult for her to work things out directly with Tim.

As Beth went further into her problem, it became clear that she was asking for the wrong kind of help because she had focused on a tangential issue. Important as it was in her mind that Tim marry her immediately, which she hoped to accomplish by a precipitous admission to the maternity home, it was more important that she understand the connection between her inability to discuss things with him and her own uncertainties about his feelings for her. With the problem redefined, Beth was able to look for solutions that would be directed toward the nub of her difficulty.

Two Interpretations of Help

Things do not always work out as smoothly as they did with Beth. Some applicants may be too resentful or depressed to participate in the interview on any but the most meager terms, limiting their responses to essentially factual information and avoiding any discussion that would impinge on relationships and feelings. Sometimes an unmarried mother cannot talk about her situation because she is not yet able to take its full measure. It is too painful to face, too demeaning to acknowledge openly. If she does not talk about it, she can, for the time being, salvage a bit of her self-esteem. At least she can spare herself some humiliation. Or she may be oppressed by a sense of guilt and responsibility. In most instances the primary crisis—the pregnancy—is of her own doing. By her own actions she has created a human being who is about to enter life socially, and possibly emotionally, handicapped.

The request for help is in itself an admission of failure—a failure in a relationship and in the resources on which people usually rely to manage their daily lives. There may have been disappointments in people on whom she had thought she could count. Her encounters with the baby's father may have been particularly disheartening. She has come to the agency anxious, depressed, or hostile, uncertain of what lies ahead for her, wondering whether the agency will give her the help she is asking for. She has to share with strangers a problem that has grown out of the most intimate of human relationships. In short, an experience that under other circumstances would have brought personal gratification and social approval has been converted into a social and psychological hazard.

Although the unmarried mother's request for help may be the agency's first acquaintance with her problem, she has been living with it for some time. She may have sought help from others and have had to answer the same questions. On being referred to an agency how many times has an unmarried mother asked, "Will I have to tell the whole thing over again?"

Certain lines of inquiry are likely to unsettle her more than others. She is apt to be particularly disturbed by questions that seek to establish her motives for becoming pregnant or that try to assess her relationship with the baby's father. Questions about how long they have been intimate or about their use of contraceptives (as one irate nineteen-year-old fumed, "Questions my best girlfriend wouldn't ask me") may strike her as unvarnished intrusions into her privacy.

An unmarried mother may learn, to her dismay, that in order to receive the service she has requested, she will have to comply with other agency stipulations. A tax-supported agency may require that she file a paternity charge against the baby's father.

An agency providing adoption service may want a direct contact with him for personal history or matching. A minor unmarried mother may have to bring parental consent before she can receive medical or social care. A maternity home applicant may be asked to commit herself to regular therapy sessions.

These terms are not what she anticipated in coming to the agency. Unable to see the connection between these procedures and her need for sheltered living, for schooling, or for help in planning for the baby, she may well be puzzled as she tries to gauge the intent of this stranger who professes to want to help her. The result may be to drive her further into her resentment and depression. Her productions may become so circumscribed that it is difficult to know whether she will ever be able to relate to the agency on any but her own terms. This kind of behavior can pose a problem for an agency. Mindful of the gap between its limited resources and the demand for them, it would like to reserve them for those unmarried mothers who are likely to make most "constructive" use of them—that is, those who will agree to its conditions of service.

From Applicant to Client—Some Unpredictables

The question is whether it is possible to assess an applicant's future behavior in the one or two interviews that usually constitute an intake procedure. Prediction in matters of human behavior is at best a tenuous undertaking. In out-of-wedlock pregnancy it is often little more than a toss-up.

Pregnancy is an experience in continuous biological change; it has its psychological concomitants. An unmarried pregnant woman may view her circumstances quite differently at seven or eight months from the way she did at three or four months. As her feelings about the baby, his father, her parents, and other important factors change, she may also feel differently about accepting help. Her reactions to the crisis induced by her having to ask for help may bear little resemblance to her behavior in later stages of her relationship with the agency and may tell very little about her capacity to change or her ability to use help.

Experience with unmarried mothers abounds in surprises. A woman who at first seemed to have ironclad defenses may, late in the pregnancy or immediately after delivery, move into problems that had been troubling her for months. It is also possible, of course, for one who came "well-motivated" to understand why she became pregnant to end up using her intellectual insights to avoid dealing with important events in her current situation. A hitherto adamant unmarried mother may decide, later, that it does make sense, after all, to involve the baby's father.

In view of these uncertainties, one must question whether a prognosis made at a point of crisis should determine the granting or withholding of services—a decision that can have far-reaching consequences for an unmarried mother and her child. It may be more important to provide her with a healing experience at this point than to try to trade an agency's services for her acquiescence to its stipulations. It can be reassuring to an anxious, hostile applicant to know she is accepted despite her need to react as she does; to know the worker understands why she cannot talk about the painful aspects of her circumstances; to realize the worker respects her need to handle things this way; and, above all, not to have to worry about embarrassing questions. The early mark of a worker's interest in her as a person can form the basis for a helping relationship and can make an unmarried mother more receptive to the agency's other requirements later, when her acute stress has subsided.

With her initial anxieties reduced, the applicant may also be more receptive to suggestions about her future. The worker can point out that although the applicant is unable to talk about some of her circumstances at this point, she will not necessarily feel this way later; that she may find herself thinking differently about the baby's father (or about the baby, her parents, or wherever her current stress is rooted) and may want later to deal with some situations differently from the way she is now doing. The worker can also explain that in some respects things will be easier to manage; that the unmarried mother may even find at times that she can allow herself to enjoy some of the good things about being pregnant and unmarried. It can be explained too that at such times she may find, as many women in her circumstances do, that it can help to talk things over with someone who has seen many such situations. Also that from a sharing of her problem she can get a better understanding of some of the things that will be happening to her, and she will be able to deal with them more purposefully and with greater confidence in what she is doing.

Such an explanation, presented matter-of-factly and undramatically, can be recognized by most unmarried mothers for what it is: the worker's attempt to help her by telling her frankly, and with the authority of experience, what it is going to be like in the days ahead—neither all grim agony nor all wine and roses. The worker offers her the hope that she is not forever going to feel as bad as she does now and that she can improve her outlook. Whether she does this on her own or with the help of the worker is up to her. The help is offered, it is explained, but the decision to use it remains her own. She thus retains a measure of control over a portion of her living at a time when much else is out of her hands, when she has to experience changes in her body and in relationships, with little power to affect what is happening to her.

It can be comforting for an unmarried pregnant woman to have some idea of what she is to expect in the coming months. It takes some of her trouble out of the realm of the unknown. If she finds later that her experiences do not differ radically from what the worker has led her to expect, her trust in the worker rises and she begins to see the worker as a source of potential help.

If, when the pressures become too much for her to bear alone, she should turn to the worker for help, she does so voluntarily, knowing what it is likely to entail, without first having to clear away obstacles to the relationship that were raised in previous efforts to weaken her resistance to help. If questions she resisted in the earlier contacts have relevance for the problem about which she is currently concerned, she will deal with them more purposefully now than she was able to at a time when she found them inappropriate and offensive, and having little bearing on what she then perceived as her difficulty.

The experience with Alice P. shows how a worker maintained a relationship with an initially hostile unmarried mother and was able to help her later at a point of acute stress.

Alice P., a twenty-five-year-old clerical worker, was five months pregnant when she applied to a public child welfare agency for help in planning for the care of the baby. She wanted to keep it, but was almost sure she would have to relinquish it. She had enough money to see her through confinement and a brief convalescence. However, she would not be able to pay for foster care should this be necessary.

In the interview she was unfriendly, almost sullen. She offered no information spontaneously, and gave only brief, factual answers to the worker's questions. She was having no contact with family or friends "until this blows over," and was not interested in speculating on how her family would react if they learned of her situation.

She bridled at questions about the baby's father and refused to give any identifying information about him, claiming it would be useless since he had disappeared shortly after she told him she was pregnant. She would not consent to the agency's trying to locate him, and the idea of her filing a paternity complaint was out of the question.

She guessed that if this was the only way the agency would help her, she would have to find some other way. She thought one of the doctors at the hospital where she worked sometimes learned of a family that wanted to adopt a baby, but she had read somewhere that it was better to use an agency. Besides she did not want anyone at the hospital to know of her situation. Yet she could not see herself going to still another agency. That would make three. She had already been to one in a neighboring town, but this agency had suggested that she try a public agency. She did not know why they could not help her. "I guess they've all got one kind of hang-up or another."

This tax-supported agency had specific regulations regarding child support from an alleged father; regulations with which Alice refused to comply. Yet it was important to keep her in contact with an agency, not only to protect the baby but also because of her own severely upset state. Her need to punish herself by inviting rejection and by isolating herself from those who could help her, coupled with her undifferentiated hostility, suggested that she had probably had emotional problems before she became pregnant. Her anticipation of rejection had been confirmed by the previous agency. She was doing her best to repeat the experience with the current agency. Another such refusal could lead to unsound plans for the baby and could do lasting damage to her.

The baby needed to be protected, and Alice needed an experience that would counteract her perception of the world as rejecting and uncaring. If the requirement about the baby's father could be relaxed, she would have help in planning for the baby and she would have tangible evidence, however limited, of the worker's concern for her.

The worker said she could understand how Alice would be angry at being given a runaround. No doubt questions about the baby's father had come up in the previous agency, and perhaps she felt it was going to be more of the same with this agency. Alice did not respond.

The worker explained the reasons for the regulation, both with regard to the law and in terms of a father's responsibility for the support of his child. She could see, however, that it was upsetting for Alice to talk about him now. The worker was not sure how long Alice could go on without filing a complaint. It would depend in part on what happened with the baby. In the meantime, until the baby was born, the worker could help her with some of the other plans she had to make.

During the next few months the worker referred Alice for part-time work and helped her find new quarters when her first arrangements proved unsatisfactory. Alice made one spontaneous reference to the baby's father in giving family history about him. "I'm telling you as much as I can. I'm amazed at how little I really know about him."

Her few references to the baby were primarily in terms of possible plans, with little talk about feeling. She was impassive when the worker suggested that with the passing of time, Alice might one day feel less bitter about the baby's father, improbable as it might seem to her now.

Although Alice's attitude toward her basic difference with the agency—the involvement of the baby's father—remained essentially unchanged, she had begun to shed some of the brittle exterior with which she had been greeting the world. She was able to respond to the worker's interest, and there were indications that she was somewhat less strongly defensive about the baby's father.

A few weeks before the baby was due, Alice asked to see the worker. She had just learned that she had a kidney infection. It was not serious, and the doctors were reassuring, but she could not help wondering whether it might hurt the baby, and it bothered her.

She asked a great many questions about adoption and expressed concern about how an adopted child might feel toward his original parents. "What do people tell the child?" The worker explained how the agency handled the adoptive parents, then said: "We can tell them some things about you. What would you like your child to know about his father?" Alice half-smiled. "Paul wasn't all that bad. I should have realized he wouldn't be there in case of trouble." She spoke of his good looks, his charm, his sense of humor, his love of fun: "Things that drew me to him because they're the opposites of what I am. They weren't much good when I needed someone with a sense of responsibility. I guess maybe he figured I had enough of that for the two of us."

When the worker indicated to Alice that she was willing to consider waiving the offending regulation, she showed she was concerned about what might happen to Alice. Alice learned to relate to a helping person and to accept the idea that she did not have to anticipate rejection from others simply because she had failed in a major relationship. She was able to turn to the worker when, under the stress of her worry about the possible effect of her illness on her child, she had to deal with certain feelings about the baby that she had previously been unable to acknowledge.

Admittedly there was an element of chance in Alice's changed attitude toward discussing the baby's father, and one cannot say whether she would have turned to the worker for help had it not been for the anxieties the kidney infection stirred up in her. On the other hand, the issue about naming the baby's father was never resolved because Alice took the baby home after a brief period of foster-family care for which she herself paid. Perhaps she would have persisted in her refusal if the issue had come to a head. This is an example of the kind of risk an agency takes when it suspends a regulation at intake in the hope that this approach will make an unmarried mother more amenable to its terms later in the contact. Is it worth the risk to waive the rules? Perhaps more cogent questions are: to what extent does it detract from the service if a given regulation is not rigidly enforced, and to what extent does it ensure a better service if the regulation is enforced?

In looking for answers to some of these questions it is well to keep in mind that there is often a quasi-protective character to an unmarried mother's need for help. If she does not receive certain basic services, her health as well as her child's may be in jeopardy. The overriding concern is that she have prompt access to the kind of service she needs for the protection of her own and her child's health and welfare. Conditions and terms of service that can present obstacles to her receiving such help should not become an issue between client and agency, and should not be grounds for refusing help on the basis of her responses in the early contacts.

A woman who is known to be pregnant out of wedlock, and who needs medical care, sheltered living, or help in planning for the care of the baby, should be able to receive it without first having to commit herself to involving the baby's father, to obtaining parental consent, or to attending psychological therapy sessions. If she has applied for a service that the agency has been authorized by the community to give, and that it is equipped by its resources to give, she should be eligible for care from that agency whether she demonstrates a readiness to accede to its additional terms or not. If an agency considers its skilled services and specialized resources essential to providing adequate service to an unmarried mother, such resources can, if they are needed, be offered to her after she has been taken into agency care.

This recommendation is not to suggest that an agency waive requirements that it is legally mandated to carry out. If it must eventually enforce terms that it is willing to suspend temporarily, the applicant should be so informed. For example, the worker did not promise Alice P. permanent immunity. She offered to see whether the requirements could be waived, but she did not guarantee that they would be.

Agency regulations can sometimes be interpreted with greater latitude than is often realized. Usually there is some leeway, a "when in the judgment of . . ." proviso by which even a legislatively established stipulation can be circumvented or waived if it is in the interests of mother or child to do so, or if it is considered harmful to enforce it.

Referrals from Others

Frequently the initial request to help an unmarried mother comes from another social agency or from someone in another profession—a pastor, a physician, an attorney, or school personnel. If the referring person is not familiar with the agency's practices, he may ask the agency to agree to conditions that are contrary to its policies. Often such a conflict happens in referrals from other professions to maternity homes, where the unmarried mother is in twenty-four-hour care, with the home acting *in loco parentis* much of the time. A physician may stipulate that a girl is not to see her baby more than once; an attorney may have plans for independent placement of the baby; a pastor may ask that the girl be required to attend chapel daily; a probation officer may ask for stricter supervision than the agency ordinarily gives.

It is important that the referring person understand from the outset the extent to which the agency can meet his requests. If the agency cannot agree to all of his requests, it should explain why not. An early understanding can avoid confusion for the unmarried mother *and* the referring person. This understanding is particularly important if the referring person plans to remain active with the unmarried mother. Often in clarifying its policy the agency can take the first steps toward establishing its relationship with the unmarried mother herself.

The experience with Sally R. is a case in point.

Sally, aged sixteen, was referred to a maternity home in a telephone call from an out-of-state physician. He had been the family doctor for years. The parents were distraught about her pregnancy, and it was important for her to leave home. He planned to place the baby with a family of his acquaintance.

The worker explained why the maternity home did not encourage independent adoptions. If Sally were admitted, it would have to be with the understanding that she would be informed of the possibility of placing the baby through a licensed agency. The agency's obligation to an unmarried mother is to help her use her concern for her baby to make the plan that is most likely to protect his future welfare. The agency has found that, in most instances, an unmarried mother is likely to prefer agency adoption.

Dr. W. was willing for Sally to be admitted with this understanding, remarking that his own feeling was that she would be more comfortable about the baby's being placed by someone the family trusted and who knew the kind of home to which he would be going.

In stating its position to the doctor, the agency made it clear to him that, since helping unmarried mothers was its area of competence as a social agency, it would have to be free to work with Sally according to its interpretation of her and her baby's welfare. This approach did not encroach on the doctor's medical relation with the family.

This case illustrates another version of the issue that came up with Alice P. The agency could have refused Sally admission on the grounds that it did not wish to be a party to an unprotected adoption. Yet this would have left her without the shelter she needed. If she came into care, she would at least have the opportunity to explore the possibility of agency adoption if she wished, free of pressure.

In the interview with Sally and her parents, Mr. and Mrs. R. expressed concern about her becoming involved with an adoption agency, knowing this would entail a certain amount of discussion about the baby. They were anxious for Dr. W. to handle it for them, since they knew he would find a good home for the baby from among his patients. "Sally knows this is best for everyone. Everything will be taken care of, and there won't be anything to worry about."

When the worker remarked that Sally had not said anything, Sally blurted out, "Does it have to be the way Dr. W. wants it?" She did not like the idea of a local family having her baby. "I can just imagine myself looking into every new baby buggy, trying to see if it looks like mine. I don't want to know it's close by. I don't want to know where it will be." Mr. R. tried to comfort her with the thought that she was upset at being in a strange place, and that she would forget about it once she got back to her friends and school.

The worker said she could understand why the parents wanted to do what they thought would be least painful for Sally. She acknowledged that sixteen did seem young for a girl to be talking about "my baby." But it was the agency's experience that young girls were often capable of handling their situations well if they were permitted to participate in the planning.

In any event, since the parents were going to be a distance away and since things do come up that sometimes have to be handled on the spot, the worker said she would have to feel free to help Sally in the way she thought best. If the worker were to promise to carry out Dr. W.'s and the parents' wishes, and then had to reverse herself, it would be confusing for Sally, and the parents would have reason to be angry with the worker. The parents agreed to Sally's being admitted on these terms, although Mr. R. still felt that she seemed "so young to be making such big decisions."

Some two weeks after Sally had been admitted, the worker telephoned Dr. W. to inform him that Sally was doing well and that she was being referred to an adoption agency at her request. Dr. W. was interested in Sally's response during the interview. "I didn't know the kid had that much spark in her. Good for her!" He asked a number of questions about the maternity home and about agency adoption practices in general, and was referred to his local agencies for further information. Six months later he telephoned to make another referral.

When an unmarried mother is referred by one social agency to another, with both having continuing responsibility, it is important that one agency be designated to take major responsibility for interagency communication. If there is no clear understanding about which one has this responsibility, it is possible that in regard to a particular problem, each may assume that the other is actively handling it. The result can then be that the client gets lost between them while important actions on her behalf are neglected. This danger must be particularly guarded against in the case of an economically deprived client who has many reality problems that require a good deal of practical planning and legwork.

Occasionally two or more agencies will vie with each other in serving a client. Such competition usually involves agencies interested in helping unmarried mothers with emotional problems, or clients whose problems appear to be interesting psychologically. In such cases it is sometimes suggested that problem areas be delineated according to each agency's function or special competence. However, the emotional gymnastics involved for the unmarried mother who is expected to classify her stresses according to agency function can be confusing to her and can prevent her from making good use of any of the agencies.

There is no single formula for assigning agency responsibility to an individual unmarried mother. My own experiences have led me to believe that if there has been a good working relationship between agencies, and if there is trust between workers (or between a social worker and another professional), and if people approach a situation with professional discipline, without competitiveness, and with respect for each other's point of view, the fine points of agency function rarely become an issue. In fact, agency function can be remarkably flexible when the primary concern is for the unmarried mother and her baby.

Intake with Unmarried Mothers Is Different

In many respects intake with unmarried mothers follows procedures commonly accepted among social agencies. It starts where the client is, it encourages her to tell her story in her own way, and it recognizes that she may need help in refocusing the perception of her need. In other respects, however, it may be necessary to depart from some of the usual procedures. Because of the special nature of the unmarried mother's circumstances, procedures that in other situations promote understanding between agency and applicant may in this case alienate her from the agency.

This departure from usual procedures applies particularly in assessing the applicant's "workability." [1] In connection with other kinds of problems, it is generally accepted that a client must manifest some understanding about the possible origin of her problem in order to participate meaningfully in solving it. Responses to such questions as, "How do you suppose this happened?" and "What do you think brought this about?" and so on, can give clues to how she perceives her problem and how meaningful her perception is likely to be in treatment.

With the unmarried mother applicant, the import of such questions often hinges on what is meant by *this*. The *this* can refer to the specific request she is making of the agency (that is, what in her situation makes it seem that shelter, adoption, and so on, will help solve her problem) or, on the other hand, *this* could refer to the condition that brought her to the agency in the first place; namely, the pregnancy.

Ambiguous as such questions may seem to others, apparently many unmarried mothers have little doubt about their meaning. I am inclined to believe that, to most of them, *this* refers unmistakably to the pregnancy. The question then boils down to (to quote one woman), "How come you got pregnant?"

Besides being upset by the question, an unmarried mother may feel that it has little relevance to her need for help. No one can do much about the thing that is bothering her most— her pregnancy. It must proceed at its own pace and run its course. It is self-terminating. Neither insight nor clarification is likely to alter it. She cannot see how knowing why she became pregnant is going to improve things for her. The most she can hope for is that the agency will help make her experience a little more tolerable than it would be otherwise.

This helplessness in the face of the pregnancy can communicate itself to other aspects of her situation, so that initially she may not perceive herself in as active a role in solving her problems as is usually expected of a client. This passivity is likely to be reinforced if, because of her dependence on the agency, she does not wish to do anything that would jeopardize her being accepted.

Many unmarried mothers do not feel they are in a position to engage in a free exchange regarding the agency's requirements or procedures. Most unmarried mother applicants need the agency much more than the agency needs them. It is an uneven match, with the power preponderantly on the side of the agency. Although the worker may strive to create a climate of joint decision-making, the applicant knows that in the last analysis it is the agency that decides whether she will be offered its services.

The Applicant Who Is Not Accepted

The intake process should include carefully-worked-out procedures for the applicant who is not accepted. If an agency decides not to grant an unmarried mother's request, she should be told tactfully but unequivocally why she was rejected. She should not have to speculate about possible reasons or wonder about agency "hang-ups" as Alice P. had to do. She should have an opportunity to react to the decision and to express her disappointment, her resentment if she can, and her concern about what is to happen next.

She should be assured that the agency means to stand by, to help her reach other sources of assistance. If she is to be referred to another agency, there should be a clear understanding, preferably before she leaves the interview and before she applies in person to the agency to which she is being referred, about the likelihood of her being accepted. In other words, she should be spared a runaround. If it looks as though there may be a succession of referrals (not unheard of among health and welfare agencies), the first agency should designate itself as an anchor service, the one to which the applicant and other agencies can report the outcome of their contacts. The anchor agency should stay with the applicant until some connection has been made where she can receive the service she needs.

It is of concern in all child welfare practice that a large number of applicants referred to other agencies do not arrive at their destinations. They join the ranks of the frequently-recorded but highly questionable intake entry: "referred elsewhere," a designation by which many not-accepted, and subsequently lost, applicants are identified. Serious as this practice may be in other types of social welfare problems, it is particularly deplorable when it involves an unmarried mother. The anxiety about whether there will be help, and the embarrassment of having to repeat her request and expose her condition to a succession of strangers can well discourage the effort to find appropriate help. It may result in poor planning, with resultant damage to mother *and* to child.

The unmarried pregnant woman whom an agency cannot or does not wish to serve should at least be of as much concern to it as is the one whom it takes into care.

NOTES

1. Helen Harris Perlman, *Social Casework: A Problem-solving Process* (Chicago: University of Chicago Press, 1957), pp. 114–30.

PLANNING
FOR THE BABY

As the pregnancy advances, the unmarried mother, like her married counterpart, becomes increasingly aware of the baby as a developing person. Increased frequency and vigor of fetal movements, dropping of the waistline, "pressure pains"—all tell her that her baby is soon to be born. At the same time her feelings toward the child become more clearly defined. Seeing him as a human being who will have to be cared for, she may become aware of her own role in planning responsibility for him. In other words, she will begin to feel like a mother toward him and is in the process of developing a maternal relationship with him.

This relationship can be the most important aspect of her experience in unwed motherhood. It involves a social and biological role that is basic for many women. It can influence for good or ill the maternal self-image with which she emerges from an experience that for most unmarried mothers is their first encounter with motherhood. Whether the plan for the baby is the result of her own decision, or whether it is due to the demands of others or to a failure in social service resources,[1] her relationship with him offers opportunities for decision-making that can tap her deepest potential for social and emotional growth. It can constitute an auspicious focus of intervention.

The Transitory Mother

The unmarried mother who expects to relinquish her baby is often in conflict between her wish to do what will be good for him on the one hand and her need to experience herself as a mother on the other. Certain questions take on urgency. Should she take care of her baby at the hospital? Will she be able to give him up if she does? Will she be sorry if she does not? Whose baby is he after she has relinquished him and before he has gone into his adoptive home? Is it selfish to keep him? If answers to these questions elude her, she may try to deny the feelings that have prompted them. But maternal feelings are not easily ignored. If she tries to deny or suppress them, she may become irritable, restless, and depressed. She may overeat or otherwise flout dietary and health regimes. If feelings about the baby's father have been reawakened, she may have a brief flurry of activity to enlist his interest. Although she may know realistically that it is a lost cause, nevertheless she needs the comfort of an "as if" game that permits her to muse on what it might be like if "something could be worked out" so she would not have to give the baby up.

At such times an unmarried mother may need help in putting her feelings into a less threatening perspective. If she knows that her feelings have been experienced by others in her circumstances, and if she can be assured that they do not inevitably spell trouble for her or her baby, she may be helped over a trying period in pregnancy. Her reactions may seem less ominous to her if she can see them as part of a natural progression of biological events that will culminate in the birth of the baby.

Often an unmarried mother who expects to relinquish her baby becomes alarmed if, as frequently happens, she finds herself reacting with strong motherly feelings following delivery. Such feelings are not what she anticipated. Suddenly everything seems to have turned topsy-turvy.

The woman who was to have no contact at all with her baby unaccountably wants to have him with her for all his feedings;

another, who was to see her baby only once before giving him up, begins to think of ways to keep him. Puzzled by feelings that would be considered appropriate in a married woman, she begins to cast about for explanations. One woman who had a long and exhausting labor says, "After what he went through, I figured he needed me. I sure needed him." Another thinks, "Because it all happened so fast, I had to see him and hold him to know that I really gave birth." A third one, dimly recalling that in an unguarded moment immediately after delivery she had asked for her baby, apologizes, "I guess I was thinking with my glands instead of my head. All my beautiful blueprints now gone straight out the window."

When an unmarried mother feels called upon to justify feelings for her child that would be approved of if she were married, she is saying in effect that she is unsure of herself in the role of mother. Pressed by opposing forces—metabolic, social, and psychological—she is confused about her relationship with her child. The biologic impact of childbirth impels her toward a physical contact with her baby. Protective and nurturing emotional impulses have been activated to match her physical reactions. Yet she is fearful that if she has a nurturing association with the baby, she will become attached to him and will not be able to give him up. Struck with her responsibility toward the new life she has created, she would like to be a good mother to him. But she does not know how a good mother is supposed to act under these circumstances. Society has not provided guidelines for the maternal behavior of the unmarried woman who is about to give up her child. Aware of the social disapproval that attaches to having a child out of wedlock, she is not even sure she is entitled to act like a mother.

Her earlier plans have suddenly become useless in the face of her new situation, and she must find new ways of dealing with this bewildering development. She has to create a different maternal role for herself. With only a few days in which she can be with her baby, there is not much time for decision-making. She is at a point of acute anxiety, in need of help, and often ready to use it. Her relationship with the baby offers an opportunity for effective intervention.

Maximizing the maternal role. If an unmarried mother (at this point she truly is, for the first time, a mother) is to use her relationship with her baby for her social and emotional maturation, she must herself experience being his mother with the approval of those who are in a close helping association with her. She must be assured that her motherly feelings for her baby are natural and proper, and that they do not necessarily derive from any inappropriateness in her emotional needs. Her maternal experience at this point should be viewed in its normal, maturational aspects rather than in terms of its out-of-wedlock, socially deviant component.

The unmarried mother should be treated like any other newly delivered mother. She should be permitted to talk about her experiences in labor and delivery; she should be able to ask questions of nurses and doctors. It is fitting for her to be proud of her baby, if pride is what she feels, to marvel at how much he eats, or to worry that he is not eating enough. Above all, as his mother, she has the right to make certain decisions that affect her relationship with him: whether she will see him once, whether she will not see him at all, whether she will give him his bottle at mealtimes. Hospital policy about the unmarried mother's association with her baby should be the same as it is for married mothers. If her decision is thought to be unwise, it should be discussed with her by the appropriate people. But unless there are clear indications to the contrary, the ultimate decision should be hers. She is legally her baby's mother until she relinquishes him, and she should be accorded the same status emotionally.

As the unmarried mother faces other decisions, she is likely to realize that she and her baby are not an island, that at some points her decisions are going to affect others who are deeply involved in her situation. If she is to act responsibly toward her baby, she must also recognize that her right to make decisions about him must be tempered by the rights of those whom her decisions affect. Her relationship with the baby becomes a bridge across which she extends her concern for him to an awareness of the needs of others.

Conflicts that arise in connection with the crisis of childbirth and the unmarried mother's relationship with the baby can produce a more accelerated receptivity to change than is found at other points of her experience. The telescoping of the maternal experience into the space of a few days lends a sense of urgency to her situation, which can cut through nonessentials and can help her to focus on the most pertinent aspects of her circumstances. Often her handling of conflicts at this point constitutes a capsule representation of her major behavior patterns in other life situations. With her psychic energy concentrated on the immediate conflict, intervention can zero in, so to speak, on the core of her stress. The focus may be circumscribed, but the ramifications can be far-reaching.

The following two cases illustrate how, through acting out the maternal role in the brief postnatal hospital period, an unmarried mother can be helped to an altered perception of herself and her life tasks.

Camilla, aged twenty-one, was six months pregnant when she entered the maternity home. She was hostile toward everyone, particularly her parents. She claimed they never had a good word for anything she did and criticized her for not having dates. On the few occasions she did have dates, they were scornful of her escorts, implying that this was probably the best she could do. As a result she had terrible feelings of inferiority and would do anything to hold on to a boy.

She thought this might be why she became pregnant. Not that she did not care for the baby's father; she just was not all that crazy about him. She knew that if she did not "make out" with him, he would find someone else.

Visits from her parents invariably ended in strong words, the parents sometimes threatening not to come again. Camilla saw no point in the worker's trying to talk to them because they would insist she was the one who had to change. As far as she was concerned, it was the other way around.

Camilla claimed to have no feeling for the baby. When she talked about him, it was mostly to complain about how long he was taking to be born, about the discomfort he was causing her, and about how unshapely he had made her. She could not imagine feeling any differently about him later, no matter what experiences others had had. To all outward appearances she remained hostile and rejecting of him throughout the pregnancy.

In an uneventful delivery Camilla gave birth to a full-term but underweight baby. When the worker visited her some thirty-six hours following delivery, Camilla was tearful and unhappy. She had seen the baby once at her own request. She wanted very much to see him again, to hold him, and to take care of him.

She could not imagine what had prompted her to ask for him. Now she kept thinking about her skinny, homely baby, figuring that he needed the individual care only she as his mother could give him. Yet she was afraid she would not be able to give him up if she were to see too much of him. She had such a good feeling when she saw him, she could have shouted with joy. It seemed wrong to be happy about something that was giving her parents so much trouble.

Camilla's reactions were compounded of normal responses to parturition, the complications of her out-of-wedlock status, and her special emotional needs. The need for bodily contact with the baby, the feeling of well-being, have been described by many newly delivered mothers. For Camilla, this "skinny and homely baby" (and he was all of that), whom she longed to nurture as she herself would have liked to be nurtured, was probably an extension of the unlovable part of herself. Her narcissism and her maternal impulses peaked in an urgent need to take care of him. But she was not sure whether it was proper to have such feelings or whether she had the right to act on them.

At this point Camilla needed to experience herself as a mother rather than as an unmarried mother. She was in effect asking the worker to approve of her wish to act like a mother toward her child. The worker could show approval, but the decision to act on her wish would have to be Camilla's.

The worker explained to Camilla that her feelings for the baby had much of their origin in functions related to parturition and that they were as natural and acceptable for her as they would be for a married woman. She thought these feelings were probably at their peak at this time and would probably begin to subside if Camilla did not have further physical contact with the baby.

Camilla was encouraged to talk about the positives and negatives involved in taking care of him. She explained that an extended contact might make the immediate separation from him more difficult. On the other hand, some girls had reported that the satisfaction of having taken care of the baby seemed to compensate for the immediate pain of separation. The worker could not predict how Camilla would react, because it is different for different girls.

Whatever she decided, Camilla would know that it was her own decision, one she had made because this was her privilege as a mother. The worker would try to help her carry out her decision so that there would be maximum benefit for her and the baby. Camilla decided to have the baby with her for feedings during the rest of her hospital stay.

In equating Camilla's feelings for her baby with those of married mothers, the worker was telling her in effect that her out-of-wedlock status did not cancel out the validity of her feelings for her child or diminish her right to make an important decision about her relationship with him. With this support, Camilla was able to move out of the impasse and to come to a decision knowing that it entailed certain emotional risks for her.

Camilla enjoyed her association with the baby and was pleasantly surprised at how easy it was to learn to handle him. It gave her a good feeling to know that something she had decided on her own had turned out well. The one thing that bothered her was her parents' refusal to see the baby. It hurt her because she would have liked to have been able to talk to them about him, but, "I guess I can't have everything."

When it was time to leave the hospital, Camilla informed the worker with some embarrassment that she wanted to have the baby with her for a few days at the maternity home.[2] She would like to be able to take care of him herself "from bath to burp." She was afraid, though, that her parents would be angry at her, and she did not want to face them with this. Would the worker please talk to them for her?

Having resolved the question of her relationship with the baby, Camilla was about to take a step she was afraid would bring her into conflict with her parents. She was torn between her wish to make her own decisions and her need for her parents' approval, and all but lost her newly-acquired confidence at the thought of their disapproval. In short, she was not sure whether her primary responsibility was as mother to her own child or as child to her parents. In order to resolve this conflict, she had to understand why it was difficult for her to face them with a decision that, on the face of it, was essentially hers to make.

With a little encouragement Camilla talked about how afraid she had always been of her father's anger. In order to avoid a face-to-face confrontation with him she would figure out ways of working around an issue, sometimes without taking the trouble to find out ahead of time how he felt about it. She had to admit she was pretty devious at times.

She would not blame her parents if they thought she was trying to trick them into letting her take the baby home. They refused to see him at the hospital because they were afraid they would want to keep him if they did. She wished she could convince them that she had no idea of keeping the baby. She just wanted a little more time with him. The few days at the hospital were just a teaser.

The worker pointed out that in this situation Camilla was no longer the little girl trying to get something for herself. Rather, she was trying to solve a problem that involved her and her child. In this capacity it would be more appropriate for her to deal with her parents herself rather than through the worker. The worker pointed out that Camilla had already made one important decision which had turned out well. Apparently she had handled it well enough for her parents to approve. Perhaps they had more confidence in her than she or they realized. The worker suggested that together they explore ways in which Camilla could present her position to her parents so that it would be acceptable to them.

Camilla apparently handled the situation successfully. The parents later told the worker that, although they were shocked and apprehensive about Camilla's taking the baby to the maternity home, they were pleasantly surprised at the calm and maturity with which she approached them about it.

The baby went into agency care following a three-day residence with Camilla at the maternity home.

The anxiety aroused by Camilla's anticipation of her parents' disapproval brought into focus long-standing difficulties in her relationship with them. Having failed in her efforts to include them in her relationship with the baby, she was moved to look at her own contributions in her former conflicts with them. She began to see them as people with needs of their own, and recognized that they had a right to make their own decisions about the baby, just as she did.

By helping Camilla to distinguish between her privileges as a mother and her responsibilities as a daughter, the worker gave further impetus to her maturation. Camilla learned that she could not be both child and adult at once, that the right to make her own decisions about the baby also entailed the obligation to deal responsibly with her parents, including, if necessary, accepting and dealing with their disapproval. As she gained confidence in her ability to make good decisions, she was able to give up the subterfuges she had previously relied on and to handle differences with her parents more directly. Thus, through a succession of decisions that were rooted in her relationship with her baby, Camilla's sense of herself improved, and she achieved a more mature relationship with her parents.

Karen, an unusually attractive woman in her early twenties, was a maternity home resident from out of state. Over the past several years she had become involved in a series of relationships that were destructive to herself as well as to others. It had become her habit to leave the scene of these near disasters before the problem could be resolved, relying on those who remained behind to pick up the pieces and deal with the consequences of her behavior.

Her pregnancy was the result of as close a relationship as she had ever allowed herself. She was never clear as to why the relationship had ended. Although she seemed at times to want to talk about her relationship with the baby's father, she was unable to pursue it with any consistency.

For the most part her relationship with the worker was one of breezy friendliness. She seemed eager for regular weekly interviews but used them mainly to recount, in sophisticated psychiatric language, a history of unhappy relationships with her parents since childhood. She had had psychiatric treatment and was intellectually aware of her pattern of "making trouble and running." However, she showed little inclination to move beyond these insights.

Her plans for the baby were carefully worked out. She had informed the worker from the children's agency that she would see her baby once after he was born and would sign an early surrender so that she could leave as soon as she was able to travel.

On her return from a clinic appointment at which she learned that she might deliver within the week. Karen spoke at length about her plans for the future. She was going to live with a college friend in another city and did not anticipate difficulty in getting a job there. All she needed now was the plane ticket.

The worker said one could not always plan so precisely when a new baby is involved. Had she talked it over with the children's worker? The agency might have some questions about her leaving the city so soon. The worker suggested also that Karen might find, after the baby was born, that she was not ready to take off so hastily after all. Women's feelings change after giving birth, and she might find herself more involved with the baby than she seemed to be now. It would be better if Karen allowed herself some margin in her planning.

Karen was nonplussed. She could not imagine what would delay her. She felt fine, and the doctors made no mention of any difficulty with the baby.

Until now Karen had managed to maintain a marginal kind of functioning, with a hit-and-run technique that had become almost second nature to her. The psychological insights and technical jargon with which she had come fortified seemed to serve only to protect her from really looking at the meaning of her behavior, particularly its implications for her approach to her coming baby. In a sense she was transferring to her baby her earlier pattern of leaving the consequences of her destructive behavior to others while she took off to distant parts. It was important, therefore, to help Karen recognize that she had an obligation to her baby and that it would be inappropriate for her to try to handle her problem in planning for him as she had done with previous difficulties.

A few days after this interview Karen asked the worker to intercede for her with the worker from the children's agency. Apparently, before it would accept a surrender, the agency required out-of-town mothers to remain in the city until it was sure the baby could be cleared for placement. Now that the worker mentioned it, Karen recalled having been told about it by the children's worker some time ago, but only in passing, and Karen had not given it much thought. This could really foul up her plans.

Encouraging Karen to deal directly with the children's agency about this question, the worker suggested that this would be a good time for Karen to give some thought to her need to "get away." Since her plans were flexible, it looked as though she wanted to leave just for the sake of being on the move. This pattern resembled so strongly some of the episodes Karen had described from the past. Could she be content to dispose of her baby as she had other problems, running away instead of facing them?

With an unhappy, "I think I see what you mean. It's a brand-new ball game, isn't it?" Karen said she would like to think about things a bit.

Karen's customary reliance on intellectual insights and terminology failed her in the face of an immutable reality—the coming baby—from which there was no escape. Now that she had to accept responsibility for planning for a child of her own creating, she could not call on the easy rationalizations that had previously served her. The anxiety this stirred up in her was the first sign that it might be possible to reach her through her feeling of responsibility for the baby.

Karen gave birth to a handsome boy a few days after the last interview. When the worker visited her at the hospital, she looked contented but subdued. She was having the baby with her for all his daytime feedings. She did not say how this had come about, but she apparently enjoyed having him with her. She spoke about his good looks, the amount he ate, and his other attributes. She made no direct reference to her feelings but asked questions about the baby's status between the time he went into agency care and the signing of surrender papers. She elected to remain in the hospital an extra day when a storm kept the children's worker from calling for him the day Karen was to have been discharged.

Karen asked to see the worker a few hours after her return from the hospital. She was depressed and said she felt terrible about leaving the baby. She wished she had not been so offhand about things all along. Bursting out with, "It's about time I stopped lousing things up and started doing things right," she said she needed help in "straightening a few things out," things that had begun to jell in her mind after that last interview before she went to the hospital.

The last two days in the hospital "things really began to hit me—hard." Each time the nurse brought the baby to her, she found herself hoping it would take a little longer for her to come back for him. She realized how completely dependent the baby was on those around him. For the first time she understood what it means to be responsible for someone—responsible and guilty. She wanted to do what she could for him, even in this short time. Maybe it would not make that much difference to him, but she guessed it was not too much for her to stay in the city until she was sure he had been cleared for adoption.

In the following weeks Karen spoke further of the way she had "loused things up" in the past few years. She realized she had been careless of the feelings of others, much as she had been at first with the baby. She was struck with the harm she had been doing herself also. Maybe it was as much her own fault as the psychiatrist's that she did not get much help before. "Maybe it's different now. All I know is, I never felt so rotten in my life."

A few months after she left, Karen wrote the worker that after a "shaky start" in therapy, she was now well involved, and "This time it really is different."

Karen's brief but concentrated relationship with her baby was the first meaningful human commitment she had allowed herself in many years. As his mother, she wanted to plan responsibly for him. Realizing that her previous ways of handling problems were not appropriate in planning for a child, she also began to question their validity in other areas of her life. She decided she would have to find other, less destructive ways of dealing with her life situations.

Uncertainties and delays. Many people question whether the unmarried mother who has taken care of her baby at the hospital is more likely to change her mind about giving him up. It is true that a number of those who change their minds have taken care of their babies. It is not certain, however, that there is a cause-and-effect relationship between the two—that is, that the mother's wavering about relinquishing the baby results solely and directly from feelings that have been aroused because of her association with him.

Women seem to change their plans for a variety of reasons. In the maternity home study, eight unmarried mothers who had originally planned to relinquish their babies changed their minds before leaving the hospital. Five had had protracted mothering experiences with their babies, two had seen their babies only once, and the other had had no contact at all. For the five, the change came about in different ways. Two women had decided late in the pregnancy to keep their babies but failed to inform the social worker. Another had intended from the first to keep her child, but had said at intake she planned to relinquish him, primarily because she thought this would be the only way she could obtain the kind of medical care she needed because of a kidney condition. In two other cases the children's grandmothers made the decision: one simply took the baby when she called for the mother; the other explained that it was inconceivable to her that an adoptive family could be found whose lineage was lofty enough to match her granddaughter's ancestry.

Of nine mothers who asked for delays in signing relinquishments after a close association with their babies in the hospital, eight subsequently released them to the agencies, and one kept hers. Seven of the eight babies were relinquished within three weeks or less.

It may be that in some instances the wavering and change of mind are the direct result of the mother's contact with the baby. It is also possible that the change in plan and the decision to take care of the baby both grow out of the same root, that the impulse to want a mothering experience with the baby may be part of the feeling that makes the mother reluctant to separate from him a few days following delivery. This feeling may be nature's way of seeing to it, in the last phases of pregnancy, that the mother will have a nurturing impulse toward her coming baby.

One must also take into consideration that at the time the unmarried mother leaves the hospital, her body may not yet be done with the nurturing function. "After" pains, enlarged breasts, even at times traces of lactation that persist despite drugs, reduced fluid intake, and binding may for some women have their psychological counterparts.

An unmarried mother who must separate from her baby a few days after delivery is in the position of having to honor a commitment she made at a time of crisis, when she may scarcely have realized that the baby would someday be a human being about whom she would care. She was agreeing then to sever, according to a future schedule, a relationship she had not yet experienced. She could not comprehend the meaning of the commitment she was making because she had no way of knowing how she would feel when the time came to honor the commitment.

Whether an unmarried mother has had a maternal experience with her baby or not, she frequently leaves the hospital with large pieces of maternal affect still active. Her body and her psyche may need time to accommodate themselves to the idea of permanent separation from the baby. Sometimes it is only a question of delaying formal relinquishment for a week or two.

The Interim Mother

Sometimes an unmarried mother may need a period of foster care for her child. Having decided to keep her baby, she may need time to make practical preparations, to arrange for housing and a baby-sitter, to find a job, and the like. She may want to look into the possibility of marriage or to explore the social climate in which she and the baby will have to live. For one reason or another, she is not yet ready to take full responsibility for his care.

During this period the unmarried mother's role as a mother is often equivocal. Although legally she may remain the child's mother and can make certain important decisions about him, in some ways she is his mother in name only. She does not perform the day-to-day functions that are a major channel of communication between infant and parent. She does not decide when he shall have a medical checkup, who his doctor shall be, and so forth. She misses the many first events that lend meaning to caring for one's child—the first cereal, the first cooing, and so forth. The frequency and timing of her visits with him are determined in large part by the agency. Often she comes to him feeling more like a visitor on sufferance than a mother, self-conscious about how her behavior toward him is being viewed.

This period can be a hazardous one for the baby, a time when temporary care can easily slip into long-time placement. In many instances the relationship with the baby has started out tenuously. Having placed him in agency care after only a brief association in the hospital, the mother has had little time to build a solid foundation to which to anchor the relationship during the separation. As the separation continues, her role as mother is likely to become more and more nominal, less and less functional. Her ties to the baby loosen; new obstacles to taking him home present themselves. Knowing that he is being well taken care of, the mother finds that it is easy to let the weeks slip by and to temporize about assuming a responsibility concerning which she may have become increasingly ambivalent with the passing of time. Her baby remains in care longer than had been planned and longer than is considered good for him.

The baby needs to be protected from the hazards of indefinite substitute care, and the mother needs to be helped to make a plan that will not impose insuperable physical or psychological strains on her. The agency is often in the position of having to mediate between the two. Sometimes it can find an ally in the mother's concern for her baby. Her wish to plan responsibly for him can move her to join with the agency toward concluding an early plan. Often this plan can be achieved in terms of a limited focus and within a specified time.

During this period the focus should be on the conditions that have made it necessary for the mother to place the baby in agency care. Besides identifying the factors that have kept her from taking full responsibility for the baby, she also has to decide what needs to be done to reduce or eliminate the impediments. Together, mother and agency can arrive at a reasonable estimate of how long it is likely to be before the mother can take full responsibility for the child, the agency offering to help where her own resources are not likely to meet her need. As they explore, from time to time, the factors that have facilitated or impeded progress toward achieving her plan, she can be helped to reassess the plan, so that, if necessary, she can either revise it or change her methods for achieving it.

When Louanna, aged twenty-three, left the hospital she was determined to marry the baby's father, as he had asked her to, and to keep the baby. After two nights of living-in with the baby at the maternity home, she asked the adoption agency for temporary placement while she and Pete looked for an apartment and bought furniture and other household supplies. It was agreed that three months would be ample time for this and that they could call on the worker for help if they needed it. Three weeks after the baby went into placement, Louanna telephoned the worker for an appointment, explaining that she and Pete were having differences about plans.

Pete was nervous and fidgety in the interview. He seemed unable to sit still, walked around the office, and talked in staccato phrases, hardly finishing a sentence. He was belligerent toward the worker, felt the agency should not push them to take the baby, and thought three months was hardly enough time to plan adequately for marriage and parenthood. He wanted time to look for a better job so he could support his family properly.

Louanna suggested at one point that Pete's present earnings were really adequate for them to start with and that there would be time enough for him to change jobs after they were settled. Other than that, she said very little through most of the interview.

The worker pointed out that they still had more than two months in which to plan and she wondered whether something else was bothering Pete about the agency's terms. Pete repeated that he just did not see the whole point of giving them only three months. He did not respond to the worker's explanation that a baby begins to recognize people by that age and that waiting too long to make the change could be upsetting for baby and parents alike. Pete terminated the interview suddenly, taking Louanna by the arm with a brief, "Let's get out of here."

Louanna came by herself for the next appointment, two weeks later. She apologized for Pete's behavior the last time and wondered what the worker's impression of him was. Did she think he was trying to get out of setting them up in an apartment together? Louanna admitted that she herself was beginning to have doubts about it. Maybe if he had more time, he would not be so nervous. Sometimes she thought it was the pressure of getting everything done at once that was bugging him.

In response to the worker's question about Pete's behavior under pressure in the past, Louanna at first insisted that she was sure this was temporary. As she talked further, however, she admitted that he had always had a temper. She had never given it much thought in the past because she had grown up with a father who had a pretty violent temper. His tantrums were really bad, but she did not think it had done her any harm. In fact, she was the only one in the family who could calm him down. She used to have to protect her younger brother, who was mortally afraid of her father, because he was the one the father would go after when he was in one of his moods.

She had always managed to handle Pete's tantrums until now, and she was sure she could continue to. Maybe if he did not feel so pushed about taking on the responsibility of a family, he would calm down. Would it be so bad to leave the baby in foster care another month? Louanna was visiting him regularly, so it would not be as though he was going to strangers when they took him.

She could not say how merely waiting a month would change Pete's feelings. She just had a feeling it might. The worker suggested that if it was only a question of time, she would be glad to help Louanna set herself up in an apartment so that she could have the baby with her. Then Pete could join them when he felt ready.

In the next interview, three weeks later, Louanna said she had decided not to marry Pete. She realized that he was not ready to be a responsible husband and father. That was what was making him so jumpy. He wanted to marry her, but she had told him she would not marry him if she had to give up the baby. He had agreed to have the baby home without really wanting it. She figured if she married Pete she would have two babies to care for instead of one, and she was not sure which would be the more troublesome. She would like to try to make a home for the baby and herself.

Louanna had started out with what seemed like a definite, workable plan for taking the baby out of agency care within a reasonable time. Problems soon emerged, however, that revealed difficulties in the relationship between the unmarried parents, difficulties that were not likely to yield to a brief extension of the deadline. At this point Louanna had had to look at the relationship problem rather than at the time limit, which she and Pete were blaming for his bad temper and which Pete insisted on extending beyond the agreed-upon date.

In talking about Pete's outbursts, Louanna recalled the fear with which her younger brother had reacted to her father's tantrums. Seeing in her own son the brother she had had to protect from her father, she began to have doubts about Pete's suitability as a father. She was able to see that the sources of Pete's behavior lay in his unreadiness for the responsibilities of fatherhood.

Having thus clarified the question of Pete's place in the plans for the baby, she now had to decide whether she would make a home for the baby by herself.

A week later Louanna informed the worker that she had decided to give the baby up. She would never marry Pete. In fact, she thought he was mentally unbalanced. She wished she could keep the baby but did not think she could make a go of it alone. He was a wonderful baby, and she enjoyed her visits with him. But the more she thought of it the more she realized she was not up to working and taking care of a baby on her own. Those two days and nights with him at the maternity home were plain hard work. What would it be like when she was all alone with him?

Actually, she had begun to realize several weeks before that this was what she was heading for. She kept trying to tell herself that she would never give him up, but the last two times she had visited him, it was as though she were visiting someone else's child. She felt terrible when she realized she was actually glad to have him in the care of someone else.

Before his birth, she had pictured taking care of a baby as all sweet, powdery smells and cuddling. She did not count on his crying half the night, messy diapers, the formula. She was afraid if she had to have him by herself, with the work and the loneliness and being cooped up, she would start resenting the baby, and in no time they would both be in trouble.

Louanna thought she was ready to sign but wanted a little more time, just to make sure she was not doing something she would later regret. She signed surrender papers when the baby was eleven weeks old.

From the point of view of mother, baby, and father, this outcome was probably as satisfactory as one could hope for. The baby was free to go into his permanent home within a reasonable time; he was spared from living with a stormy and unstable father and possibly an unhappy mother. The father was not saddled with a responsibility he was ill-equipped to undertake. The mother was satisfied that she had exhausted all possibilities in planning for the baby and that she had made a responsible decision. When she relinquished him, it was probably with less anguish than she would have felt had she not been able to satisfy herself that she had arrived at a decision on the basis of a careful consideration of the important elements in her and the baby's situation.

One of the important factors in Louanna's readiness to assess Pete as a potential husband and father was that she knew she would have to terminate the temporary care arrangement at the specified time. She also knew that the time limit had been arrived at on the basis of the baby's well-being. The worker did not deviate from the deadline, because it was evident that extending it would not have altered the basic deterrent to the parents' removing the child from agency care; namely, the unmarried father's unreadiness to take on the role of permanent father. By adhering to the time limit the worker was able to help Louanna recognize the unsoundness of her original plan.

Although a time limit can be useful, it should not become an end in itself. At best it is only one of several elements to be used in helping an unmarried mother plan for the care of her child. If a time limit dominates the planning, removing the baby from agency care on schedule can become a primary objective, at the expense of other, more important considerations. Moreover, enforcing a time limit does not automatically guarantee that a child will be better off than if he remains in continued substitute care.

When an unmarried mother is required to come to a decision about her baby at a specified time, she usually does one of two things. She either releases him for adoption or removes him from agency care and makes her own provisions for him. My impression from limited data is that, for some reason, unmarried mothers seldom relinquish their babies when they have to conclude a plan under pressure from an agency. They are more apt to remove the child from care, often making plans that are considerably more hazardous than continued placement would be. The ultimate cost in human waste may in the long run be considerably greater than continued supervised agency care would be. The money the community has saved by terminating placement may eventually have to be expended several times over to repair the damage that can result from improper care from the mother.

For example, in the study of maternity home residents,[3] it was found that of six mothers who had been asked by child-placing agencies to remove their children from care at the expiration of deadlines that ranged from six weeks to three months only one relinquished the child—but not until she had had him with her in a furnished room for four weeks. The others made the following arrangements: one mother placed her baby in day care with an alcoholic neighbor while she worked; another came to the attention of the agency when she was arrested for larceny, at which time it was learned that the child had been in three different foster homes in the two months he had been in his mother's care; two had made stable arrangements for the care of the child; and the sixth had been lost sight of.

There are times when, in order to protect the child from a more hazardous arrangement, placement may have to be extended beyond what would ordinarily be considered advisable. Often it involves an emotionally disturbed mother who, although psychologically incapable of assuming responsibility for the baby, refuses to relinquish him. In such situations, treatment for the mother may have to take temporary precedence over a time limit.

Cora, aged twenty-six, entered the maternity home six weeks before her baby was due. She hoped to marry the baby's father, but realized it had been hopeless all along. She planned to relinquish the baby and was already in touch with an adoption agency.

With the birth of the baby, after a protracted and exhausting labor, Cora found herself "caught in a vise." She felt strangely remote from him, as though he were unreal, but realized he was a handsome, good-natured baby. She wanted to have him for all his daytime feedings, yet she could not summon any genuine tenderness toward him. She felt unworthy as a mother and besmirched as a person, with nothing to offer a child. Nevertheless, she could not promise to abide by her earlier agreement with the agency that she would relinquish him on leaving the hospital.

The baby went into foster-family placement while Cora went home to convalesce. She was to see the child-care worker weekly while she tried to decide what to do. She visited the baby faithfully every week, but according to the foster mother, her approach to him was emotionally antiseptic. She did the right things for him on instructions from the foster mother, but was stiff and awkward, almost mechanical in the way she handled him. There was usually an air of depression about her during these visits.

It became evident in the first few interviews that Cora was not going to reach a decision quickly. She dwelt on her feelings of inadequacy as a mother, and her guilt at keeping the baby in foster care. After two months she was still unable to mobilize herself to make a home for him or to release him for adoption.

Here was an apparently damaged young woman who could neither relate to her baby nor allow him to go into an adoptive home. One of the purposes for which she seemed to be using him was to perpetuate her perception of herself as degraded and unworthy. In some ways she seemed to gain satisfaction from this image of herself. Indications were that she would be many months making up her mind. One of the questions for the agency was whether to set a date beyond which it would not keep the baby in foster placement.

In psychiatric consultation it was suggested that Cora's perpetual self-accusations were protecting her from having to relate to the baby and hence from having to conclude a plan for him. It was not known how much of her reluctance to become involved with him was due to lack of feeling for him and how much might be due to displacement of feeling from the baby's father. Reinforcing this reluctance, however, was a sense of incompetence she felt because of her unfamiliarity with babies.

It was difficult to know how tenuous her psychological balance was, what vulnerabilities would suddenly be exposed, and where the strengths lay. Any approach, it was felt, was full of risks. But some steps had to be taken to move her off dead center, a position that was doing neither her nor the baby much good. It was felt that efforts to uncover underlying problems at this point would fix her defenses more rigidly and might unsettle her psychologically. It was decided, therefore, to deal with the problem that was accessible and familiar to her; namely, her plans for the baby's future. It was thought preferable, for the time being, not to press her with a deadline, but to deal with the question in as relaxed and congenial an atmosphere as possible.

If after a trial period Cora could gain no satisfaction from her association with the baby, the agency would be in a stronger position to take a firm stand about his need for more stable living arrangements. If she decided she could function satisfactorily as a mother, she would be helped to arrange to remove him from agency care. At that time the possibility of a time limit could be considered. The expectation was that Cora would soon recognize that she was not ready to assume the practical and emotional responsibilities of motherhood and would relinquish the baby. It was a long shot, and it did not work.

The worker talked with Cora about being more active in the care of the baby so that she (Cora) could get a better sense of her feeling about her relationship with him and thus would have a sounder basis for deciding whether she wished to relinquish him or make a home for him. Cora immediately construed this as pressure from the agency (which in fact it was). She burst out angrily about the "side issues" people were impressing on her—her parents' social status, her father's professional standing, community opinion, a quick plan for the baby—everything except what was happening to her. All they could see was that she was the baby's mother. Didn't she count herself?

The worker agreed that Cora had reason to feel pressed. She wondered, however, whether Cora could really separate her feelings about herself as a person from the way she felt as the baby's mother. She herself had been expressing concern about what would happen to him with this protracted period in foster care. Yet in not letting herself act as the baby's mother, and in failing to do what she felt she should, she was perpetuating a poor sense of herself as a person. She did not have to become more active with the baby if she did not want to, but it seemed too bad not even to give it a try.

Cora had a good relationship with the foster mother. With the latter's encouragement she became more relaxed with the baby, more deft in her handling of him, and more responsive to his needs. She was particularly proud when she took him for a two-hour visit to her mother's without mishap. She spoke of him more frequently and spontaneously to the worker.

Most of her friends were understanding of her situation, and she anticipated no difficulty in re-establishing social contacts. When the baby was four months old, Cora made it clear that she meant to keep him. Before taking him out of agency care, however, she wanted time to find an apartment and arrange for his care while she was at work. She wished she could stay on with her parents. Her mother would like to take care of the baby for her, and it would be wonderfully convenient. But knowing her mother, the baby would turn out to be her mother's child rather than her own, and she did not want to have to cope with that problem right off.

For good or ill, Cora had come to a decision. Whether it was a sound decision is moot. On the plus side, she began to relate positively to the baby and manifested other areas of strength. On the minus side, there was still potential trouble. Hints of conflict with her mother existed, and her feelings about the baby's father were still largely unresolved. The effect on her relationship with the baby could be serious.

Whether the agency approved of her decision or not, there was no alternative at this point but to support her in it and to help her carry it out with as little harm to herself and the baby as was possible under the circumstances. The way had to be kept open for her return to the agency if she encountered unmanageable problems later.

Cora admitted to being fearful about her decision. She knew it would not be easy to bring up a child by herself, but she was not giving up the idea of marriage. She wondered whether she would be inclined to marry the first man who asked her, out of gratitude that he would be willing to be a father to someone else's child.

When the worker suggested that perhaps Cora was also thinking of being grateful for someone's wanting to marry her after she had had an out-of-wedlock child, she admitted that this had been on her mind ever since she had decided to keep the baby. Although it was better now than it had been when he was first born, it still bothered her when she was feeling low or uncertain about things. What bothered her most was the way she used the baby when she first decided not to give him up.

It was a blind decision because she had no intention at that time of ever taking him home. It was as though, when all were badgering her about their own concerns, and she was too guilty and confused to answer them, the baby was her only weapon for getting back at the people at whom she was furious—her parents, the baby's father, the social worker. She knew this was a terrible way to use a child, but she could not stop herself. "I think I was as close to being crazy those two months after Alan was born as I'll ever be."

In subsequent interviews Cora talked further of her feelings about the baby's father and the effect they might have on her relationship with the baby. She realized there were pitfalls ahead and that the real test would come after she had taken the baby home, but she also knew she could return for help if she needed it. For the time being, she preferred to try herself out on her own.

On the recommendation of a friend, she had arranged with a middle-aged widow to care for the baby while she was at work. Cora removed the baby from agency care when he was seven months old.

Cora had made substantial strides by the time she was ready to take the baby home. She related positively to the baby and seemed comfortable about herself in the maternal role. She had gained some useful insights about herself and had an improved sense of herself as a person. She had had a positive experience in receiving help and had a good relationship with the agency worker, to whom she could later turn if she needed help.

The experience with Cora raises a question regarding the

limits of substitute care. How long does an agency continue a child in care before it decides enough is enough? At what point does it designate itself the child's advocate and try to secure an involuntary surrender from a mother who cannot decide one way or the other, whose psychological status is so poor that the child's welfare is in danger of becoming submerged in her own drives.

Susan K., aged twenty-nine, applied to a child-placing agency when she was five months pregnant. She was planning to keep her baby, but thought she would need a brief placement for him while she worked out plans to establish a home with the baby's father.

She had been treated for psychological disturbances in the past and gave a history of poor work experiences and fragmented personal relationships. A previous marriage had ended in divorce, as a result of which she had lost custody of her only child. She was currently living in a furnished room which, according to her own description, was "more crowded with empty beer cans and cigarette butts than with furniture."

Except for her relationship with the baby's father, she was socially isolated and she depended on him for all her affectional and social needs. Their two-year association had been characterized by intense quarrels and intermittent separations which alternated with equally intense reconciliations. Nevertheless, there were many positives in the relationship, and they needed each other.

According to Susan, she had contrived the pregnancy in order to force Ned into divorcing his wife and marrying her, something he had been promising for the past eighteen months, but had always put off.

In the early interviews Susan was flip and gay, almost manic. She was optimistic about setting herself up in a household with Ned even if he did not divorce his wife. She tried to engage the worker in parrying psychiatric concepts, and dwelt at length on the relation between her current emotional instability and her parents' mishandling of her during her childhood.

This was an obviously disturbed woman who was involved in a pathological relationship with the baby's father. Her sense of the realities was quite tenuous, as was evidenced by her plan to establish a family-type menage with the baby and his father.

It was clear from the outset that if the baby went into agency care, it would probably turn into a longtime placement.

In consultation with her most recent psychiatrist it was decided that insight-oriented treatment was not indicated. Her earlier experiences had been amply gone into in previous treatment. Warming over the emotional trauma she had suffered at the hands of her parents served, in her mind, primarily to justify her erratic behavior. Susan was going to have to live through, step by step, the realities she would have to face in learning what was going to be feasible for her and the baby. It was thought she should have a structured living arrangement to protect her health and the baby's, and she readily accepted referral to a maternity home.

Susan's stay at the home was stormy. She was given to hysterical crying spells, particularly after visits from Ned, and occasionally would go off overnight without informing staff that she planned to be away.

After the baby was born, she changed her mind about placing him. She returned to the maternity home with the baby so that she could look for an apartment and arrange to take him directly with her. Staff reported that she took good care of the baby at first and responded sensitively to his needs. She handled him lovingly and seemed to get great satisfaction from her association with him. However, her interest began to flag after a few days. She became forgetful about his routines, was slovenly about the room, careless about the baby's laundry, and so forth.

Ned was a most reluctant father. In a joint interview he was alternately lukewarm and hostile to the idea of setting up house with Susan and the baby. He could not maintain two households, and to leave his wife now could wreck his professional career.

When the worker later asked Susan what she thought Ned meant during the last interview, Susan admitted momentarily that maybe she was seeing the handwriting on the wall. However, she soon comforted herself with the explanation that his reaction was no more than "the usual male panic" at realizing he was actually a father. After all, this was his first child. She was sure his fears would subside if she could only involve him in some sort of family life with her and the baby.

A few days later, Susan announced that it looked as though she was going to have to force the issue with Ned. She would take the baby to a furnished room. Ned would then realize that she meant business, and he would have to take some responsibility for them. Sooner or later he would grow to love the baby, if only from seeing him and providing for him, and he would then be ready to move in with them.

Susan's plan to take the baby to a furnished room was the first sign that he could be in jeopardy if he was in her care. She was now seeing him as a means of forcing a response from the baby's father. Although she was scarcely in a position, financially or emotionally, to take on the responsibility for his care, she was unstable enough to carry out her threat.

At this point she was legally free to plan as she wished. The only way to protect the baby was to keep her from taking him with her while she was in her present precarious state financially and psychologically. Moreover, if she could be freed from responsibility for the baby, she could look for a job and an apartment, and could investigate baby-sitting possibilities unencumbered. Despite the risk of possible longtime placement, this plan seemed, under the circumstances, to be the least of several evil alternatives.

Susan accepted the suggestion that the baby go into agency care with apparent relief. At first she visited him weekly in the foster home, occasionally accompanied by Ned. She kept biweekly appointments with the worker.

The worker did not question Susan's attachment to the baby or challenge her motives in wanting to keep him. She supported the positives in her feelings for him and occasionally used these feelings to elicit concern about the possible ill effects of his remaining in care too long. The worker also helped Susan through many stormy episodes with Ned. Susan was alternately hostile toward and protective of him and clung to slight evidences of his interest. She was unrealistic about possible financial contributions from him and about her ability to supplement them with her own earnings.

When the baby was ten months old, he was moved to a second foster home because of the illness of the first foster mother. Although he eventually weathered the move, he had several weeks of crying and poor sleep in the new home. Susan remarked on his reaction to the change in placement. She was concerned that he not go through it again but was optimistic again when she saw him return to his customary sunny disposition.

With the baby's reaction to his first relocation, Susan was getting the first evidence of what continued placement could do to him. She was concerned enough to care about it. She was also secure enough in her relationship with the worker for the latter to deal more directly with Susan's unrealistic hopes about her future with Ned.

The worker explained that the older a child gets, the more upsetting relocation is likely to be for him, and the longer he remains in foster care, the greater the risk of relocation. Perhaps it was time now to consider more stable plans for the baby. She pointed out that Susan had long been trying to arrange to have the baby with her with not much luck. What chance did Susan think there was of making a home for him, with or without Ned?

Susan guessed there was nothing to do but face the fact that Ned did not want to be a father to the baby and that he was incapable of acting decisively about a divorce. She began to question whether she herself had it in her to sustain the committed relationship a lifetime of raising a child demands, particularly if she had to do it on her own.

Susan became quite depressed as she questioned whether her love for her baby was as meaningful as she had thought it was. Yet her feeling for this child was so much stronger than what she had experienced with her other one. It seemed to reflect the warmth she had felt in her relationship with Ned. Now she was not sure any more.

She had begun to realize a few months before that she was probably little more to the baby than another visitor. He was friendly when she came and seemed to recognize her quickly. But for comfort and security he invariably turned to the foster mother. She had been feeling differently toward him, too, more remote, less involved. As time passed, it became easier to skip visits. She thought if she could have him with her again, she would be able to recapture the joy she had felt at being with him in the first days at the maternity home.

Susan's self-interest and her concern for her baby combined to make her think seriously of releasing him for adoption. Although her relationship with the baby had some meaning for her, it was not strong enough to take precedence over her need for Ned. Recognizing that continued placement would not be good for the baby and that perhaps he was at this point more of a hindrance than a help in relation to Ned, she was ready to consider relinquishing him.

The worker remarked that this change in Susan's feelings about the baby did not take anything away from her earlier experiences with him, nor did it indicate that those feelings were not real at the time. A mother's feelings for her baby were likely to diminish with prolonged separation. The worker supported Susan in her concern for the effects of foster care on the baby and introduced the question of a date for relinquishment.

Susan accepted the idea that ultimately she would probably have to give the baby up. Perhaps it would even improve her chances of restoring her relationship with Ned if she were not constantly hounding him about his responsibilities to a baby he had not wanted in the first place. Susan signed relinquishment papers when the baby was eighteen months old.

This situation was about as precarious as can be found for an out-of-wedlock child. It was unlikely that Susan would ever be able to function adequately as a mother. One could not in clear conscience try to enforce a time limit that might have led her to take the baby out of agency care. The alternative—to try to secure an involuntary surrender—is often not promising. The procedures required and the probable outcome are likely to discourage voluntary agencies, sometimes tax-supported agencies also, from taking necessary action.

Definitions of neglect, abuse, exploitation, and other forms of parental incompetency are often subject to the interpretation of whoever happens to be sitting on the bench at the time. Moreover, investigations, continuances, and postponements can so prolong the proceedings that there may be a better chance of having the child surrendered by persuading the mother to relinquish him voluntarily than there would be by waiting for a court decision, particularly if there is no assurance that the decision would be favorable to the child. As the experience with Susan suggests, there may be times when the best protection for a child is for the agency to keep him in care, staying with the situation and applying palliatives to reduce the damage to him, while trying to motivate the mother to release him voluntarily.

The relationship with the worker can be a major factor in helping a disturbed unmarried mother arrive at a sound decision about her baby and to recognize that she will probably have to give him up. If, in the preceding months, she has experienced the worker's concern for her as well as for her baby, she is more likely to listen when the worker raises the ultimate question.

If the worker has not challenged her right or denigrated her capacity to make decisions, there are no straw men to tilt at. If the worker has not confronted her immediately with a deadline, she has not had to rivet her attention to the passing of time, wondering whether she will be able to meet the deadline and curious about what the worker will do if she does not. Perhaps more important than these considerations is the fact that she can turn to the worker for support and comfort when her relationship with the baby collapses. For example, Susan's relationship with the worker sustained her for many months after she relinquished the baby.

The Ongoing Mother

The unmarried mother who knows from the first that she will be taking her baby with her from the hospital does not have the sense of urgency about her relationship with the baby as does the mother who faces early separation from her baby. The first mother has plenty of time. In fact, the sobering thought that this is forever can dampen the elation that often comes with successfully delivering a baby. In this she is at one with many of her married counterparts.[4]

As an unmarried mother, she must now think of how, single-handedly, she is going to discharge her responsibility to the life she has created. She is not sure she is up to it. She may have doubts about her capacity for good mothering and about herself as a person. If she dared, she might admit that sometimes she wishes she did not have to keep this baby, particularly if her decision was more by default than by choice, as is often the case with Negro unmarried mothers.

These feelings, emerging in late pregnancy, have taken on added urgency with the advent of a flesh-and-blood baby. Knowing that mothers are supposed to love their babies, the ambivalent mother may feel guilty about these reactions and may later try to deal with them in ways that could be harmful to the baby.

Because she is unmarried, she is vulnerable to any intimation that confirms her own suspicions that she may be less than worthy as a mother. She is likely to be particularly sensitive to those who represent official society—doctors, nurses, social workers, teachers, and others who may be in close association with her during pregnancy and lying-in. The way a nurse hands her the baby, the way a doctor answers her questions, whether she is in fact encouraged to ask questions, can help establish a better image of herself as a mother, or they can reinforce feelings of unworthiness.

The unmarried mother who is to keep her baby may need help in understanding and accepting her ambivalence toward herself and her baby as a normal part of being a new mother. These questions often lend themselves to group discussions as part of health education classes. As she learns, with other members of the group, about the physical changes taking place in her and the fetus, she can also learn about the psychological components of prospective motherhood, particularly as they are affected by the complications introduced by the out-of-wedlock status. Such classes, located in a maternal and infant care center, in a hospital clinic, in a settlement house, or in some other accessible setting, can promote a relationship between the mother and the agency that can be a source of help when she has to cope later with the day-to-day tasks of taking care of her child.

NOTES

1. For studies of factors associated with the plan for the baby, see: Ruth Rome, "A Method of Predicting the Probable Disposition of Their Children by Unmarried Mothers," *Smith College Studies in Social Work,* 10 (March 1940), pp. 167–201; Jane S. Hosmer, "Traits Predictive of the Successful Outcome of Unmarried Mothers' Plans to Keep Their Children," *Smith College Studies in Social Work* 12 (March 1942), pp. 263–301; Henry J. Meyer, Wyatt Jones, and Edgar F. Borgatta, "The Decision by Unmarried Mothers to Keep or Surrender Their Babies," *Social Work* 1 (April 1956), pp. 103–9; Charles E. Bowerman, Donald P. Irish, and Hallowell Pope, *Unwed Motherhood: Personal and Social Consequences* (Chapel Hill: University of North Carolina, 1963), pp. 187–236; and Clark E. Vincent, *Unmarried Mothers* (New York: Free Press of Glencoe, 1961), pp. 203–41.

2. This maternity home was one of a rapidly vanishing few that provide for a brief joint residence of mother and baby. Latest reports indicate, however, that this trend is again reversing itself, with several maternity homes reporting in the past year that they are accommodating mothers and babies in joint residence.

3. Bernstein, "One Hundred Unmarried Mothers and Their Problems," unpublished study (Boston: Crittenton Hastings House, 1961–63).

4. For a discussion of the reactions of first-time pregnant married women during pregnancy and the early postnatal period, see Florence E. Cyr and Shirley H. Wattenberg, "Social Work in a Preventive Program of Maternal and Child Health," *Social Work* 2 (July 1957), pp. 32–35.

4

AFTERMATH

One of the principal tasks for an unmarried mother following the conclusion of a plan for the baby is to divest herself, psychologically and socially, of her identity as an unmarried mother and to incorporate her recent experiences into her day-to-day living. Relationships with family members, with the baby's father, and with friends may have to be realigned, and decisions about work, school, and living arrangements made. Inextricably interwoven with these tasks is the unmarried mother's perception of herself in her new status as mother. Although the broad issues underlying this adjustment may be similar regardless of the plan for the baby, the form the problems take and the methods of coping with them are likely to depend upon whether a woman has released her baby for adoption or kept him.

Post-Separation Experiences

The unmarried mother who has relinquished her baby has to accommodate herself to the loss of a child she knows to be alive, and whose loss in most instances signifies the abrogation of her maternal role. She has to translate the fleeting experience she had as a mother into an ongoing image of herself as a mother to children she may have later.

The following discussion is based on post-relinquishment contacts with unmarried mothers who were known to a maternity home and to two voluntary child-placing agencies.[1] In most instances the first postpartum contact was not planned ahead of time, but came about when the woman returned for a postpartum checkup or to sign relinquishment papers. Each of the women had at least one face-to-face interview. Several returned subsequently for further help. Personal contacts with all but Susan K. were terminated within three months of relinquishment, although additional information was received later in letters and telephone conversations. There was no predetermined plan regarding the number, frequency, or timing of contacts. They were arranged with the unmarried mother according to her need. No effort was made to obtain corresponding information for purposes of comparison from the many who did not initiate contacts with the agency.

It is recognized that information based on such limited contacts does not warrant generalizing about the aftermath experiences of unmarried mothers who have released their babies for adoption. However, there were enough similarities among many of those seen to suggest that there may be a broad pattern of psychological post-separation response that can form the basis for further study. If common elements can be identified from these experiences, it might be possible to develop methods for helping unmarried mothers anticipate some of their later reactions so that they can be prepared to cope with these reactions if and when they should occur.[2]

On the basis of contacts with unmarried mothers who returned to the maternity home following their discharge from the hospital, and of reports from those who were seen subsequently, the immediate post-separation reaction can best be described as a confusion of feelings: relief, though not to the degree anticipated, that the pregnancy was over; feelings of physical emptiness coupled with psychological aimlessness; and a sense of unreality about having had a baby. Some unmarried mothers were frankly depressed, and not much given to talking except in snatches here and there; others were restless and agitated, and seemed to look for things to do to keep themselves physically busy. The much-looked-for return of the flat abdomen and the prospect of resuming normal activities seemed, at the moment, hardly to compensate for the pervasive sense of loss. Many envied the prenatals; a few were fleetingly hostile toward them for still having their babies safely with them. There were also doubts. Some unmarried mothers, although maintaining that taking care of the baby at the hospital had been worthwhile, now wondered whether they would have felt so bereft if they had not done so. Those who had had only brief contact with their babies reproached themselves for not having given the babies a more loving start in life and wondered whether themselves had missed something. Many of the mothers asked where their babies would be, what their status would be, and the like. Those whose babies had not been called for by the time they left the hospital were upset at the thought that their babies would be in a kind of limbo, with no one person specifically responsible for them. They did not welcome reassurances that they would forget in time. At that point they wanted to remember, not forget.

Subsequently most reported that acute grief lasted from a few days to two or three weeks. There was no designated period of mourning, and most began to resume their day-to-day activities almost immediately upon returning home. However, many hesitated to become involved in social activities—parties, dances, new dates. They seemed to have to avoid having fun for a time.

Following this period there was a time of mixed reactions, during which grief episodes were less frequent, less anguished, and briefer. One of the chief complaints about this period was that there was no way of knowing when grief reactions would recur. Often they would take a woman by surprise, sometimes in the midst of a relatively tranquil, even happy, period. Occurrences that would have gone unnoticed under other circumstances would suddenly drive home an irrevocable sense of loss.

One young woman, while looking for work, "happened" to wander through the infants' wear section of a local department store and was overcome with grief at the sight of pregnant women buying layettes. Another, who had decided to settle in the area after relinquishing her baby, had a massive grief reaction after the excitement of locating and furnishing an apartment and finding work had died down, and she had "settled in."

The birth of a friend's or sibling's child apparently can have similar effects.

Maternal feelings for the baby took a sharp drop six to ten weeks after separation. For many this change in feelings was accompanied by guilt and self-doubting. Some found it difficult to accept the idea that they missed the baby less, that they were able to lead a relatively normal life and were, in fact, having fun again. It was particularly upsetting to some not to be able to recall what the baby had looked like. A few tried to work out psychological devices to keep the baby's image fresh in their minds.

Some women questioned the substance of their earlier feelings for the baby, wondering whether they were emotionally superficial, incapable of meaningful and lasting feelings, and therefore not likely to be good mothers to children they might have later. For example:

What bothered Frances most was that she was losing her feeling for the baby. How could she feel so remote from him after having loved him so much? She had been awake when he was born, and she felt that she would never forget the excitement of it. Maybe she was kidding herself about loving him those few days at the hospital. "Maybe I was just in love with the idea of having a baby." Yet the elation and tenderness she felt for him then certainly seemed to be the real thing.

Every once in a while now, right when she was in the middle of a good time, she would suddenly think of him. Partly she missed him at such times, but mostly she thought she *should* be missing him, as though there were something wrong about having fun so soon after giving up one's baby. "It's like I'm grieving because I'm not grieving any more." Sometimes the only way she could make herself remember what he looked like was to imagine herself feeding him at the hospital. Sometimes even that did not work any more. Did her reaction mean her feelings did not go very deep if she could forget so easily?

As the maternal ties with the babies loosened, some mothers again turned to questions about their babies' future welfare. There were renewed questions about the child as an adopted child, many of which had already been asked and answered before the babies were born. How is it decided which adoptive parents shall receive which child? Will he be told that his parents were not married to each other when he was born? Underlying these questions seemed to be each mother's concern about her child's opinion of her as his mother for having given him up, the question of whether people would explain things to him so that he would understand why she had to relinquish him.

At this point many mothers seemed to need to recapitulate the whole experience. They talked about their pregnancies, their experiences in labor and delivery, and their babies. They marveled at the miracle of gestation and birth as enthusiastically as any married woman. Some said it was hard to resist chiming in when married women were recounting their experiences in pregnancy and childbirth, and many times they were tempted to blurt out something about their own.

This reliving of the earlier experiences seemed in some ways a prelude to leave-taking, a summing up of the joys and pains of something through which they had lived; an effort to fix some aspects of it in mind, to discard others, and to reassure themselves that, although all of it had indeed happened to them, it was now appropriate to finish this chapter and to look to the future. Some of them seemed to need the worker's approval to terminate the relationship with the baby, much as they had earlier asked approval to experience a mothering relationship with him. They needed to be reassured about the correctness of this emotional separation.

In reality, there is probably no such thing as total termination of the relationship with the baby, except in rare instances. It is rather that, in time, most women come to view it in a manageable perspective, each in her own way and in relation to her special circumstances. The opportunity to talk to a trusted, sympathetic person—her mother, a sibling, or a friend—can help a woman over some of the more trying moments. No doubt, some are left with scars.

A brief review of the later status of some of the unmarried

mothers discussed in preceding chapters indicates possible outcomes of the post-relinquishment experience.

Ten months after relinquishing the baby, Louanna was working, taking evening courses, dating, and "talking to my mother like I never did before." She missed the baby, sometimes acutely, and had a very bad time when his birthday came around. However, she felt the worst was over, and she did not regret having given him up.

A letter from Camilla a year after she left the maternity home reported that she had just terminated treatment with a family agency to which she had been referred in her home city. She was about to be married to a young man "who even my parents are crazy about."

Dorothy continued in psychiatric treatment. Although she was doing well at work and with social relationships, she was unable to relate to men except on the most superficial level. She continued to be plagued by thoughts of the baby and was fearful that if she allowed herself to become involved with a man, she would become pregnant again.

Susan, who had continued her contact with the agency, went steadily downhill. When last heard of, she was on the verge of being hospitalized.

Does the nature of the prerelinquishment association with the baby significantly affect an unmarried mother's aftermath adjustment? If so, is she better or worse off for having had a nurturing relationship with him before separating? Unfortunately, information is too scattered and unsystematic to provide the basis for any firm conclusions. My own impression is that, although the immediate pain at separation may be more intense for some, the long-run outlook is more favorable for most women who have had a satisfying maternal association with their babies before giving them up. It apparently brings a sense of well-being and fulfillment that expresses itself in such observations as: "For the first time in my life I knew what it was to be glad I was a woman" . . . "I had a nice baby and I took care of him at the hospital. I'm glad I did. He'll always be my first baby. I don't intend to shout it from the rooftops, but if anyone asks me, I'll tell them" . . . "It's a sad feeling a lot of the time, but it's a satisfied feeling too."

This anecdotal information, although quite revealing about the experiences of some unmarried mothers is not sufficient to support a theory. Invariably the failures crop up to challenge a hypothesis. An unmarried mother may have a physical association with her baby at the hospital and still have difficulty in the aftermath period. Sandra B. is a case in point. Four weeks after the baby had gone into agency care she was, to all outward appearances, doing well. She enjoyed her job and had good relationships socially and with her parents and siblings. However, a low-keyed malaise kept her below par psychologically.

Sandra could not understand why she should have been so reluctant to sign the surrender. She did not think she was all that attached to the baby. She had enjoyed taking care of her, and she was proud to have such a pretty baby. But she could not say she felt like much of a mother to her, except for the day before she was to leave the hospital. She did not know why, but things were different that day. Each time they brought the baby, she felt they were bringing her own baby, not just a pretty thing that she had happened to give birth to.

She wished she had felt more love for her baby from the first. That one day was just a teaser. "Now I don't know how I feel. Not sad, really. Just edgy, as though I don't know what to do with myself. The whole thing is still like a dream. It seems as though I'm signing away something that was never really mine."

Admittedly one cannot attribute all of an unmarried mother's post-separation reactions to her experiences with her baby. The supports she receives from important people in her environment, the social climate in which she must function, her economic circumstances, and her general physical and psychological predispositions—all may have a great deal to do with the way a woman copes with this problem. At present we do not have instruments for measuring the intensity of maternal affect or for predicting how persistent its aftereffects are likely to be. There is no timetable by which all women can be expected to have resolved their post-separation problems. We do not know what psychological effects the seemingly voluntary nature of the surrender of the baby may have as compared with situations in which separation from the baby is due to outside forces, such as death or a medical condition.[3] These important areas in the unmarried mother's experiences merit a good deal more attention in research than they have been receiving.

Despite the paucity of information, some measures can be taken to help an unmarried mother weather some of the postrelinquishment stresses. One way is to prepare her for possible post-separation reactions. Many women were as much upset by the thought that they were reacting inappropriately at the time, and that their reactions therefore signified psychological trouble, as they were by the reactions themselves. This suggestion corresponds to the approach mentioned earlier for preparing the pregnant woman for possible reactions to the birth of the baby. If a woman does not have to worry about the ominous implications of her feelings, if she is not taken by surprise by them and can understand why she is experiencing them, she is apt to be in a better position to cope with them if they should arise. Having advance information gives her an opportunity to take the measure of what she can expect later, to test her capacities for dealing with her aftermath reactions, and on this basis to determine whether she will need help.

Whether an unmarried mother who further needs help returns for it may depend in part on what she thinks such help is likely to entail. Her experiences with the agency during the prenatal period often color her perception of the postpartum contact. Perhaps it is not an exaggeration to suggest that in many instances an unmarried mother's attitude toward prolonging her association with the agency or resuming it postpartally is determined long before the baby is born and that more often than we realize follow-up care starts at intake.

The Unmarried Mother and Her Child in the Community

The unmarried woman who keeps her baby has to establish herself and her child in the community as a family unit. She has to provide for the child's economic and material sustenance, and give him the emotional nurture he needs for healthy psychological growth. She has to establish a perception of herself as an adequate mother.

How does the solo unmarried mother apply herself simultaneously to the tasks of provider, parent, and homemaker? What problems does she face in carrying out these tasks? What substitutes does she find for the supports that are available to other mothers? How much of an influence on the adjustment of mother and child is the fact that in many instances they are continuously identifiable as an out-of-wedlock family?

Findings from three follow-up studies of unmarried mothers who kept their children form the basis for much of the following discussion.[4] Where appropriate, they are supplemented by additional material from two studies that deal both with unmarried mothers who kept their babies and with those who released theirs for adoption.[5] Although the studies deal with different sizes and types of population, and in the areas investigated, and although they vary in the rigor of their research methods, the aggregate of the findings points up some of the common experiences unmarried mothers are likely to encounter when they undertake to raise a child singlehanded.[6]

One of the more consistent findings was that, for most of the women interviewed, having an out-of-wedlock child did not entail severe social penalties. It did not result in poorer family relationships or bring censure from friends, neighbors, or colleagues who knew about their circumstances.

There was no evidence in the study that any of the women had been stigmatized by the out-of-wedlock experience to the extent of its interfering with their further development. Most of the married women told their husbands about [it].[7]

The vast majority of unwed mothers report that their friendship relations remained stable. . . .[8]

The baby was credited with having brought some of the women closer to their families but others said the baby had an opposite effect. The most common response, however, was that the baby had made no difference.[9]

... only 9 [out of 80] said that some of their friends had cast them off. . . .[10]

The great majority of the women did not feel their chances for marriage had been seriously prejudiced by their having had an out-of-wedlock child. Many were married at the time of the interview, either to the baby's father or to someone else. Very few women had tried to conceal the child's birth status by calling themselves "Mrs.", by moving out of the neighborhood, or through other subterfuges. These findings included, besides blacks and Puerto Ricans, white middle-class women, a group that has hitherto been considered particularly vulnerable to the social hazards of illegitimacy.

Approximately half continued to live in the same neighborhood as before [the] birth of [the] baby. This was true in a greater measure for white than for Negro mothers. . . . A larger per cent of the middle class than of the lower class were living in the same neighborhood. . . .[11]

... only a few . . . made any attempt to conceal their status. . . . Only one had moved to a new neighborhood. . . . [The lack of problem in this area] was not limited to one cultural or economic group.[12]

Whether social acceptance is as widespread as these findings suggest is not certain. The data have to be viewed in the context of those who were available for study. Considering that those interviewed represented from 27 to 52 per cent of the original target populations, it is possible that those who were not available were the ones who were not faring well or who felt there would be social penalties if they were identified as unmarried mothers.

The tasks of day-to-day living. By and large, the findings regarding unmarried mothers who kept their babies were not spectacular.[13] For the most part the women seemed to be neither outstandingly competent nor abysmally inept as mothers. They managed reasonably well, their lives consisting of the routines that constitute daily living for millions of American mothers of young children. The vast majority retained personal responsibility for their children and gave them adequate physical care. On the basis of limited observation and information, the children seemed fairly well off emotionally and psychologically.

About 60 to 80 per cent of the mothers were managing financially, deriving their income from their own earnings, from contributions from their families, or from the baby's father. Sixty to 80 per cent had never received public assistance at any time prior to the study interview. Most lived in adequate housing. Several of the mothers had married, a few having already been divorced.

There were also difficulties however. Different studies showed that from one- to two-fifths of the families lived in poverty, with several others scarcely above the nationally defined poverty line. Two-fifths had had to rely on partial, intermittent support from public assistance at some time prior to or including the study period. Many who should have had supplementary assistance from the public agency did not apply because they did not want to involve the baby's father and also wished to avoid red tape, or because they assumed, from previous experience or from hearsay, that having an out-of-wedlock child would make them ineligible or would present other difficulties.

Poor housing, the handmaiden of poverty, plagued from one-quarter to more than one-half of the families at some time prior to or during the study period. Overcrowded deteriorating buildings, rat and vermin infestation, and lack of central heating or a private bathroom were not uncommon. A number of mothers moved from place to place, sometimes living with the babies in furnished rooms, trying to find livable and inexpensive quarters. In several instances, having an illegitimate child made them ineligible for public housing.

Many mothers complained of being tied down, with accompanying depression, loneliness, and boredom. There were problems in personal relationships and social adjustment. Some expressed the need to talk with someone about their child, wanting to get help in learning to care for him, puzzled about what to tell him about his father. A few interviewers noted problems that the mothers did not mention. Occasionally a woman would confide to the interviewer her longing for male companionship.[14]

The Working Mother

Between 30 and 50 per cent of the mothers worked at some time prior to or including the study period. For the most part, however, they were able to work only intermittently and part time, many of them encountering difficulties even with limited work schedules. Very few were able to support themselves entirely from their own earnings. From time to time a mother would have to stop work because the baby was not thriving or because baby-sitting arrangements had broken down. Few, if any, had access to subsidized day-care services or could afford licensed commercial day-care centers. Practically all the mothers relied on private arrangements—family, friends, neighbors, or paid baby-sitters. Many had makeshift arrangements which had to be changed when difficulties developed.

The following reports illustrate some of the problems unmarried mothers ran into in trying to arrange baby care while they worked.

"I am trying to find a night job, like cleaning offices, because my sister could watch the baby at night. I don't have anyone right now to watch the baby during the day so I have to stay home. I do not want to leave him with strangers."[15]

"Carlos [the putative father] lost his job, so I left the baby with him. He would drink and not watch the baby properly so it didn't work out."[16]

Four months after the baby's birth the unwed mother moved from her own mother's home to that of the putative father's mother. Shortly thereafter she began working and left the baby in the care of the putative father's mother, paying $10 a week for this. When the baby was six months old, the unwed mother moved to her own apartment and made arrangements with a neighbor to take care of her infant for the same amount of money. The unwed mother was dissatisfied with the care this neighbor gave her baby and once more asked the putative father's mother to tend the child. However this arrangement also proved unsatisfactory—"I only saw my baby on weekends and I felt I was neglecting him," said the woman. "Also traveling back and forth was tiring." At the time of the last interview with this woman she had made still another child-care arrangement with a new neighbor, this time for $15 a week.[17]

Lack of training, education, or experience prevented some who would have liked to work from finding jobs, or kept the earnings of those who did work too low to allow them to be entirely self-supporting. A small proportion stated frankly that they preferred to stay home, particularly while their babies were young. In other words, an unmarried mother's decision to work or stay home with her child is likely to rest on the same considerations that influence any unsupported mother, whether she be widowed, divorced, or separated.[18] The availability of adequate, inexpensive, and conveniently located day-care services; fatigue; the satisfactions of working outside the home; financial gains or liabilities; the physical and psychological consequences for herself and the child—all must be taken into consideration in any mother's decision to go to work.

Unfortunately, the resources necessary for a sound decision are available to few unmarried mothers. Yet the public temper seems to demand increasingly that the unmarried mother who would otherwise be dependent upon public financial support be "encouraged" to work, particularly if her children are of school age. Coupled with offers of appropriate educational and vocational training for the mother, "workfare" proposals are designed to reduce the number of families receiving support from the Aid to Families with Dependent Children program. The idea is not new. Beginning in the late 1940s and continuing through the early 1960s,[19] there was a rash of demonstrations across the country designed to prove that many AFDC mothers could be motivated to go to work and that the saving to the taxpayer thus effected would be considerable. Many mothers, among them sizable numbers of unmarried mothers, did indeed go to work. Many of the projects concluded that not only was it feasible for the mother to work, and that the mother's working did not necessarily jeopardize the family's well-being, but also that it could actually result in improved family relationships, in that the mother could come back refreshed from contact with adults and from having experiences outside her own home. And no doubt this did happen in a number of situations.

However, there was a striking lack of comment in most of the reports about the long-term effects of case closings when the mother lost her job and had to reapply, with the customary wait between application and reinstatement of the grant. More remarkable was the absence of information about the kinds of arrangements made for the care of the children while the mothers were at work. The few reports in which child-care arrangements were discussed revealed that the mother's working could sometimes constitute a hazard for the child. In one instance, a nine-year-old was responsible for the care of her two younger siblings. In another, the mother, unable to find daytime care for the children, worked at night, figuring that they were safer in bed at home by themselves than they would be unsupervised on the streets. In still another, the children were allegedly under the remote supervision of a neighbor who promised to "look in" on them from time to time after school.

In other words, an unmarried mother's working, as does any unsupported mother's, involves considerably more than her simply finding a job, with or without special training. If a "workfare" program is to achieve improved conditions for the recipients of AFDC, as it is expected to do, it must be applied with regard for the circumstances of the individual mother and child, and must provide the supports necessary to make the mother's working a constructive experience for her and her child.

In this connection, the growing interest in mother-baby living arrangements, as are found in England, Denmark, Sweden, and other countries, offers hopeful possibilities for meeting some of the problems of the unsupported mother, unmarried as well as others. These programs provide low-cost shelter and meals, scaled to the mother's ability to pay. The child is cared for while the mother goes to school or work, and the mother assumes varying degrees of responsibility for household tasks depending upon individual circumstances. As an interim arrangement, it gives her an opportunity to get on her feet before establishing herself independently with her child.

Help with the mothering role. An unmarried mother, particularly if she is a new mother, may need help in moving into the mothering role. It takes time for some women to make the transition from the role of newly delivered mother, cared for and free of responsibility at the hospital, to her function as the mother of a baby who is suddenly supposed to be the center of her interest. The early weeks of caring for a new baby can be trying under the best of circumstances. In a study of first-time married mothers, for example, it was found that, for the first weeks at home, "feelings about motherhood and parenthood were to a large extent parent-centered rather than child-centered. Many of these young parents seemed to need time to adjust to their own roles before they could think in terms of the child rather than of themselves." [20]

For the unmarried woman who must carry the responsibility singlehanded, it can be discouraging. From time to time the thought of her child's birth status may trouble her. Consequently, she may be quicker to interpret as deficiencies in herself or the child problems that are not uncommon for new mothers and babies. Behavior that can alarm any timid first-time mother— fretfulness, poor sleep, digestive troubles, strange grimacing— may, to her, be evidence of her incompetence as a mother. Tension, loneliness, and fatigue may make her resentful, and she may get off to a poor start in her relationship with her baby.

If she is living alone, or if she does not have strong supports from family or friends, she may need supplemental help. Sometimes a week or two with a homemaker, or frequent visits from an understanding public health nurse or a community aide, may be sufficient to help her through the first tasks of getting to know her baby and of learning to manage formula making, feeding, and the endless diapers and household tasks that go with a flesh-and-blood baby.[21]

In later weeks, the interest of staff at a maternal and infant care clinic can help her with the ongoing mothering tasks. Problems in her relationship with the developing child can be recognized early and dealt with less threateningly in such a setting than in one that focuses primarily on her role in producing the difficulty. Many women who avoid seeking help from agencies that are primarily problem-oriented or because they did not like their prenatal agency experiences can often accept it in connection with a "normal" service. Problems about child care can be woven into the conversation about eating, sleeping, changes in diet, and the like, and can be dealt with as a normal part of child development rather than as evidence of the woman's shortcomings as a mother. If she can have approval for the things that are going well and does not have to be ashamed or defensive about the care she is giving her baby, she is more likely to give herself to a relationship with the helping person, whether it be nurse, nutritionist, social worker, pediatrician, aide, or other staff person. On the basis of such a relationship, she is more likely to be inclined to examine, if necessary, attitudes and actions that may need to be modified.

An unmarried mother who establishes such a relationship can have someone to turn to for help when she begins to think about explaining her child's parentage to him. Many women who have not been defensive about the child's birth status at first become troubled as he grows older, wondering how to explain the absence of a father so that it will not harm him. According to a number of practitioners, many mothers become uneasy about this problem in connection with registering the child for school. Some mothers have noted that, although the question is likely to remain quiescent until then, they think the child senses at an early age that there may be something different about his paternal origins. Uncertain about how to handle it, the mother encourages a conspiracy of silence between herself and the child until it is forced into the open by something he has heard from his playmates or by an official event like registering in school.

An unmarried mother's reluctance to discuss the child's father with him may sometimes indicate that she, too, has unresolved questions about her own relationship with the father. In the process of helping her explore ways of handling the child's status with him, she can sometimes be helped with these questions in relation to her own feelings.

The quality of a mother's parenting often reflects her estimate of herself as a person. In turn the value she places on herself frequently mirrors society's perception of her. A chronically discouraged unmarried mother who feels society does not care enough to provide the ingredients for safe and dignified living for herself and her child may find it hard to be a loving mother. Yet public officials who administer the resources that are ostensibly intended to strengthen family life can contribute to its breakdown by imposing on unmarried mothers eligibility criteria that may not be required of others. When one considers the restrictions that are often placed on services for unmarried mothers who keep their children—housing, financial assistance, schooling, and even, in some instances, health care—one cannot help being impressed that so many of them manage at all. Time and again one has the impression that an unmarried mother would probably manage well with her child if her out-of-wedlock status was not made the fulcrum on which important official decisions hinge.

For example, the behavior, and hence the eligibility, of an unmarried mother who applies for AFDC may be judged by criteria that are not applied to people in other categories of public assistance or to other mothers. Child neglect in her case may be broadly interpreted in terms of her sexual behavior, actual or rumored, regardless of the quality of her parenting or the condition of the child.

Such an interpretation can lead to the ridiculous kind of situation that was found when a judge ruefully admitted that the child before him was indeed well cared for and well disciplined, that he was receiving good religious training and was in fact getting from the mother all a community could ask for in the way of decent upbringing. However, because the mother was unmarried and was "keeping company," he had no choice but to adjudge her unfit. She could choose between losing the AFDC grant or having the child removed from the home and placed by the state in foster care. To the judge's relief, the mother chose to keep the child and lose the grant. Apparently it is not considered detrimental to a child's welfare to remain in the care of an "unfit" mother as long as the state does not have to pay for it. Or is it more moral for the child and the mother to go hungry than for the child to be supported by the state in the home of an "unfit" mother?

Raising a child singlehandedly is at best a difficult job. For many unmarried mothers there are added strains. Yet, because a woman is an unmarried mother she is often prejudged to be less capable of coping with the strains of single parenthood than are those whose single parenthood has resulted from the death or desertion of the father, or from separation or divorce. Society often approaches her in a way designed to make sure its assumption about her incompetence is fulfilled. Nothing could more effectively nullify the original intent of the Social Security Act and its many subsequent amendments, which was to strengthen family life by making it possible for a fatherless child to be taken care of in his own home.

In most respects, an unmarried mother's need for community help stems not so much from having had an out-of-wedlock child as it does from her having the same problems that married mothers have. She may need public housing not because of some mysterious ingredient in her marital status, but because she cannot afford private housing. She may need day-care services because, like many working and unsupported mothers, her earnings do not allow her to provide safe substitute care for her child. She may need public assistance because, like other poor people, her income is inadequate for her and her child's needs. She may need a helping hand and emotional support because, like other solo parents, she carries the burdens of parenting and homemaking unassisted.

In sum, an unmarried mother needs the same creature protections we all do: security of income, and enough of it to enable her to house, feed, and clothe herself and her child adequately and in dignity. She also needs male and female companionship, and fun and relief from drudgery. She needs to be able to look to a better future for herself and her child.

NOTES

1. Rose Bernstein, "One Hundred Unmarried Mothers and Their Problems," unpublished study (Boston: Crittenton Hastings House, 1961–63), pp. 129–32.

2. It should be noted that except for information about housing, employment agencies, and help with school re-entry, none of the unmarried mothers who released their babies mentioned pressing practical problems. This probably reflects in part the greater maneuverability of the woman who relinquishes her baby, the more advantaged circumstances of those known to maternity homes and voluntary child welfare agencies, and the bias of the interviewer concerned with the maternal experience.

3. See David M. Kaplan and Edward A. Mason, "Maternal Reactions to Premature Birth Viewed as an Acute Emotional Disorder," in *Crisis Intervention: Selected Readings,* ed. Howard J. Parad (New York: Family Service Association of America, 1965).

4. Helen R. Wright, *80 Unmarried Mothers Who Kept Their Babies* (Los Angeles: Children's Home Society of California, 1965); Mignon Sauber and Elaine Rubinstein, *Experiences of the Unwed Mother as a Parent: A Longitudinal Study of Unmarried Mothers Who Keep Their First-Born* (New York: Community Council of Greater New York, 1965); and Ellery F. Reed and Ruth Latimer, *A Study of Unmarried Mothers Who Kept Their Babies* (Cincinnati: Ohio Department of Public Welfare, 1963).

5. Charles E. Bowerman, Donald F. Irish, and Hallowell Pope, *Unwed Motherhood: Personal and Social Consequences* (Chapel Hill: University of North Carolina, 1963); and Dorothy Levy, "A Follow-up Study of Unmarried Mothers," *Journal of Social Casework* 36 (January 1955), pp. 27–33.

6. The study populations were as follows: Wright, 56 per cent

white, 25 per cent black, the remainder Mexican or Indian; Sauber and Rubinstein, 87 per cent black or Puerto Rican, 13 per cent white; Reed and Latimer, 66 per cent white, 34 per cent black; Bowerman, Irish, and Pope, 60 per cent black, 40 per cent white; and Levy, predominantly white former maternity home residents.

7. Levy, "A Follow-up Study," p. 33.

8. Bowerman, Irish, and Pope, *Unwed Motherhood*, p. 306.

9. Sauber and Rubinstein, *Experiences of the Unwed Mother*, p. 50.

10. Wright, *80 Unmarried Mothers*, p. 30.

11. Reed and Latimer, *A Study of Unmarried Mothers*, p. 49.

12. Wright, *80 Unmarried Mothers*, p. 30.

13. Data for these findings are reported as follows: Wright, *80 Unmarried Mothers*, pp. 19–23, 25, 41, 51; Sauber and Rubinstein, *Experiences of the Unwed Mother*, pp. 81–84, 107–8, 126, 135–37; and Reed and Latimer, *A Study of Unmarried Mothers*, pp. 19, 22, 23, 32, 38, 41, 46.

14. Reed and Latimer, *A Study of Unmarried Mothers*, pp. 38, 40; Sauber and Rubinstein, *Experiences of the Unwed Mother*, pp. 66–79, 133–34; and Wright, *80 Unmarried Mothers*, pp. 60, 67, 89 ff.

15. Sauber and Rubinstein, *Experiences of the Unmarried Mother*, p. 99.

16. *Ibid.*, p. 101.

17. *Ibid.*, p. 121.

18. U.S. Department of Health, Education, and Welfare, *Children of Working Mothers*, prepared for the Children's Bureau by Elizabeth Herzog (Washington, D.C.: Government Printing Office, 1960).

19. This summary of AFDC demonstrations is a digest of part of a report submitted by Elizabeth Herzog to the Committee on Unmarried Mothers, U.S. Children's Bureau, May 27, 1963, in connection with a review of research and demonstrations pertaining to unmarried mothers.

20. Jane E. Paterson and Florence E. Cyr, "The Use of the Home Visit in Present-day Social Work," *Social Casework* 41 (April 1960), p. 187.

21. Aline B. Auerbach, "Meeting the Needs of New Mothers," *Children* 2 (November-December 1964), pp. 223–28; and Elizabeth P. Rice, "Social Aspects of Maternity Care," *Obstetrics and Gynecology* 23 (February 1964), pp. 307–15.

5

THE ADOLESCENT
UNMARRIED MOTHER[1]

In many respects teen-age unmarried mothers face the same tasks as do other unmarried mothers. However, factors peculiar to this developmental stage often present special problems in diagnosis and treatment. The pregnant adolescent, married or unmarried, must deal simultaneously with two developmental tasks that ordinarily would have occurred in sequence and would have stretched over several years. Biologically, her body has to cope with the stresses of pregnancy before it has accommodated itself fully to the demands of puberty. Psychologically, she has to cope with the adult tasks of motherhood while still acculturating herself to the problems of adolescence.

In contrast to the married teen-ager, who in most instances becomes legally emancipated at marriage and who is likely to have social support in the exercise of the adult role when she becomes pregnant, the social role of the unmarried pregnant adolescent remains ambiguous. As a minor, she is legally under her parents' control. In many states she is not permitted to marry, relinquish her baby, or receive medical care without their consent. Thus, although biologically about to become a mother, she is socially a dependent child, prevented from making decisions that are ordinarily considered part of parental rights and responsibilities.

Such is the paradoxical framework within which the adolescent has to work out her problems as an unmarried mother. She needs to effect some reconciliation between the opposing roles, to express her needs as an adolescent while moving toward a responsible adult role. The problems engendered by this conflict will be discussed in connection with three major areas: the relationship with the baby and parents, health care, and education.

The Relationship with Baby and Parents

The conflict between the adolescent and adult roles often emerges sharply in the teen-ager's relationship with her baby. The pregnancy forces her to give up many of her cherished adolescent activities. In most instances she is required to leave school. Gradually she loses contact with most of her contemporaries and becomes more and more dependent on her parents.

Lacking the support of her peers, and denied the customary physical and social outlets for her impulses, she has to find other ways to emancipate herself and establish her own identity. For the duration of the pregnancy, the only way open to her is through her role as mother. Questions of authority, of limits, of self-determination, and of decision-making, which she would normally work out with her peers by way of dress, dates, and cultural and social values, now have to be resolved through decisions about her baby, the baby's father, and the like. Often these issues bring her into conflict with her parents.

Many adolescents and their parents are able to weather the stresses of out-of-wedlock pregnancy without outside help. Through a critical experience, sympathetically shared, mother and daughter are particularly susceptible to a rapprochement during this time. An adolescent's distress, coupled with her need for a positive, nurturing relationship with a mother person, often evokes a protecting response in her mother. This sort of response may constitute a spontaneous turning point in their relationship. Identified with each other as mothers, the communication that opens up between them in this area frequently extends to other aspects of their relationship. The often heard, "I never felt so close to my mother before," and the answering,

"For the first time I can talk to my daughter like to another woman," attest to the potentials for family reconciliation that reside in the crises of adolescent unwed motherhood.

In some instances, however, parents and adolescent are unable to resolve their differences without help, particularly if severe antagonisms existed between them before the girl became pregnant or if aspects of her behavior puzzle or alarm the parents. Although the struggle between them can sometimes be bitter, the tensions that threaten to tear them apart may also contain the seeds of reconciliation. For, along with their antagonisms, there also is a need to make restitution to one another.

The parents, although angry and hurt at what their daughter has done, may also be worried that this experience may harm her. Indoctrinated by the popular shibboleths of the day, they think they have failed as parents and feel responsible for what has happened to her. They recall the many sins of omission and commission that they think contributed to her pregnancy. Now and then it occurs to them that they will be grandparents to their daughter's out-of-wedlock child. They wonder how grandparents are supposed to act under such circumstances. They are groping to find a way through this dilemma, to see themselves as good parents.

The girl, on her part, may also want to repair some damage. Despite her adolescent resentment toward her parents, she needs them now. She is troubled by thoughts of her own transgressions against them, particularly those that may have contributed to her pregnancy. Mindful of the pain she is now causing them, she would like to reinstate herself as a good daughter.

As a family unit or subunit, they are susceptible to intervention and change, much as an individual can be at points of crisis. Subcrises that erupt around specific issues can become the instruments for improved relationships. The social worker is in a position to help.

Because time is short and issues are likely to be urgent, the helping person must move in quickly to cut through the charges and countercharges that are often made in such situations and that can divert attention from the main question. Without dis-

couraging the expression of anger, which at times may be necessary to clear the air, the worker should focus major attention
on the baby's welfare and on the tasks the adolescent and
parents must face if they are to keep from making him the
victim of their hostilities.

Early in the contact, preferably in a joint session with the
adolescent and her parents, there should be an understanding
about the ground rules, so to speak, by which they and the
worker are to be guided in subsequent contacts. The tasks the
adolescent and her parents must face, both vis-à-vis each other
and in relation to the baby's welfare, need to be identified.

A major task for the parents is to help their daughter use this
experience for her emotional and social maturation, which means
that, in the course of a few months, they must alter their perception of her from that of child to that of mother and responsible adult. They must shift their relationship with her from
parent-child to almost a peer relationship. This change cannot
happen at once. It is a difficult adjustment for parents. There is
likely to be a good deal of backing and filling before they can
accept the idea that their teen-age daughter can have positive
maternal feelings for her child, that he is not necessarily just a
doll to her, and that she may be capable of making responsible
decisions. Often the focus of conflict is not so much whose
decision is better but, rather, who has the right to make it.

The adolescent, on her part, needs to understand that things
cannot go entirely her way; that although certain decisions may
be hers to make, others belong to her parents; and that the
privilege of making decisions carries certain responsibilities,
one of the more important of which is that she not shift to others
the consequences of decisions she herself has made.

As the worker crystallizes the issues, she engages adolescent
and parents in an implied agreement; namely, that each must
reckon with the feelings of the other while the worker must
respect the feelings of parents and adolescent alike. If chronic
relationship problems have been stirred up or aggravated by the
girl's out-of-wedlock pregnancy, they can be dealt with in terms

of the critical decisions that must be made in planning for the baby.

Parental Involvement. The case of Holly S. illustrates how a chronic relationship problem between an adolescent and her mother, aggravated by the out-of-wedlock pregnancy, was improved through the handling of crises it stirred up.

Holly S., aged eighteen, was seen with her widowed mother when she applied for admission to a maternity home. She was five months pregnant. The understanding was that the baby would be relinquished for adoption.

The two were in open conflict from the first. Mrs. S. accused Holly of being deceitful and a troublemaker. Holly blamed her mother for never trusting her, always holding her responsible when things went wrong without bothering to get the facts. Much of the quarrel revolved around Holly's relationship with the baby's father, although each dipped into the past to marshal further evidence of the other's offenses. Apparently one of Holly's ploys was to bait her mother into making a decision for her, then blame her for interfering in her affairs if things turned out badly. Mrs. S. invariably went for the bait.

After entering the maternity home, Holly was often in trouble with staff and residents. She was remiss about daily chores, yet would volunteer for extra assignments, which she invariably failed to carry out. She could not tolerate success and always managed to manipulate situations to her own detriment when things were going well for her, sometimes causing trouble for others as well. The worker saw her frequently during this period, much of the contact focusing on her need to manipulate people and her need to fail, as well as other aspects of her adjustment in the home.

After two stormy months, Holly began to improve in behavior and in relationships in the home. She was more relaxed during this time, and there was a brief respite from quarrels with her mother. The respite was short-lived, however. In a few weeks she was again in trouble in the home, had battled fiercely with her mother, and seemed bent on destroying her relationship with the worker. She was alternately provocative and withdrawn, and finally practically defied the worker to stop seeing her.

The worker pointed out that Holly was showing the kind of

tension many girls do as they come closer to delivery, particularly if they expect to give the baby up. No doubt Holly was having trouble managing her feelings. Most girls find it helpful to talk about it when they feel this way. Holly did not respond. The worker told her that so long as she (the worker) was there and as long as Holly wanted to see her, she would continue to see her. "Maybe, Holly, you ought to stop working so hard trying to get me to reject you."

Mrs. S. was seen separately several times. She used the interviews partly to talk about her personal problems, partly to express her concern about Holly's propensity for getting into trouble. She became particularly concerned when, toward the end of the pregnancy, Holly became quite uncommunicative with her. Mrs. S. was sure there was something fishy about it and had a feeling Holly was hatching some plan about keeping the baby that would end up with Mrs. S.'s having to take care of it for her. She admitted that perhaps there was something to the worker's comment that Mrs. S. sounded almost as though she would be disappointed if Holly did not impose on her as she expected, and began to discuss her need to have Holly make a martyr of her.

Holly's pregnancy highlighted and intensified a relationship problem with her mother that had existed throughout her adolescence. Their pattern of suspicion, mutual provocation, and accusation expressed their deep need for each other. It was evident that Mrs. S. would probably be involved in many of Holly's important decisions and that help for Holly would depend to a large extent on Mrs. S.'s readiness to let go of her. On the basis of past experience Mrs. S. had reason to be chary of Holly's possible machinations. Yet she seemed unable to protect herself from them and in some ways seemed to invite this treatment from Holly.

There was no way of knowing what Holly was up to. Perhaps she did have some idea about keeping the baby. If she did, it would not be unusual for someone at her stage of pregnancy. No doubt she had reason to think that if she tried hard enough and long enough, she could eventually get her mother to do what she wanted.

Whatever was brewing between Holly and her mother, they needed to understand what each was contributing to perpetuate the unhealthy elements in their relationship, and they needed to be prepared for the possibility that there would be open trouble after the baby was born. It was also important for the worker to clarify her position at this point so that Holly and her mother would understand that the worker could not be caught up in their hostilities.

The conflict between Holly and her mother erupted in a joint interview shortly before the baby was due, during which accusations were particularly acrimonious. The worker pointed out that with the baby's birth so close, tensions were bound to run high for both of them. There were going to be some difficult times after the baby was born also.

The worker said she would like to be as helpful as possible to both Holly and Mrs. S., but she could do this only if she did not take sides in the battles between them, and if she did not allow herself to be used by one against the other. She could understand why Mrs. S. might suspect Holly's intentions. However, Mrs. S. could not be forced to do anything she did not wish to do. Furthermore, the worker was not ready, merely on the basis of past behavior, to assume that Holly meant to use the baby to manipulate Mrs. S. If Holly was having second thoughts about giving up the baby, she would not be the first to feel this way. This was something she would have to work out in terms of her concern for the baby.

At this point, the conflict between Holly and her mother had to be refocused in terms of its possible implications for the plan for the baby. Both had to understand that if Holly was thinking of keeping him, there was some validity in her feeling because of the stage of the pregnancy. The worker also introduced the idea that on the basis of her concern for the baby, Holly might realize that it would be inappropriate for her to use him to manipulate her mother. On the other hand, Mrs. S. had to recognize that the decision about the baby was essentially Holly's to make and that Mrs. S. would be manipulated by it only to the extent she allowed herself to be.

Holly gave birth to an unusually handsome baby. By the time he was a week old, she had made a succession of decisions, each of which denoted a tightening relationship with him. She ordered pictures of him, she decided to have him with her at all his feedings at the hospital, she had him baptized, and she asked for several weeks' foster-care placement for him pending the outcome of an anticipated visit from the father. As Mrs. S. noted, "She talks adoption, but she acts like she expects to keep him." With each decision Holly and her mother became embroiled in a new crisis. Mrs. S. saw each new move as part of Holly's design to involve her with the baby to the point where she would be trapped by her own love for him and would want Holly to keep him, knowing it would end with Mrs. S.'s taking care of him.

At first Holly asked the worker to plead her cause for her each time she decided something she knew would upset her mother. She soon recognized, however, that the struggle with her mother was basic in their relationship, that if she was serious about her feelings for her baby and if she really wanted a better relationship with her mother, as she said she did, she would have to work these things out herself. If Holly was sure of her own motives, perhaps eventually she would be able to convince her mother that she only wanted her to share her love for the baby and that she was not trying to trap her into anything.

Holly showed increased maturity with each new decision. She began to realize that until then she had given her mother no grounds for having confidence in her. She became more open about her feelings. She could not honestly promise she would not keep the baby, because she really did not know. The only way she could keep him would be if she and George married. This was yet to be decided.

Holly was depressed after the baby went into foster care. "I really don't know what I want. It seems if you get to love someone for real and you want to do for him, you have to lose him anyhow, so what's the difference. But at least this time I'll tell it straight how I really feel."

Holly admitted that she had hoped, through her handsome baby, to get the recognition from her mother that she seemed unable to achieve for her own sake. She guessed maybe she did have it in mind to use him in a way. Yet she loved him and did not want to do anything that would hurt him. Whether she kept him or gave him up, she would like to be the kind of mother he would be proud of.

Shortly after returning home Holly went to work and enrolled in evening courses.

Holly was at a turning point in her perception of herself as a responsible human being. She could either resort to her old patterns and use the baby for her narcissistic needs, perpetuating through him the conflict between her mother and herself, or her love for him could become an avenue for her own emotional growth.

For her part, Mrs. S. had to learn that Holly's attitudes toward her were not unalterable, that she had already shown a readiness to grow. However, Mrs. S. had to accept Holly in a different role. She would have to let Holly make her own decisions and her own mistakes. She had to decide, in essence, whether she really wanted a better relationship with her daughter.

Mrs. S. and Holly were seen in a joint interview some two weeks after Holly had gone to work. At first there were the usual accusations and counteraccusations. Each blamed the other for the impasse they had come to in deciding about the baby. Mrs. S. accused Holly of enticing her into seeing the baby so that she would be trapped by her love for him. Holly blamed her mother for not telling her what to do and thus making it so much harder for her to decide on her own. She accused her mother of having never trusted her, and now she had no confidence about the rightness of anything she wanted to do. Mrs. S. and Holly both ended in tears, scarcely looking at each other.

The worker remarked that Holly and Mrs. S. seemed to be caught up in their love for the baby. Neither wanted to take the responsibility for saying he should be relinquished. Each was trying to put the burden of the decision on the other. The worker pointed out that this argument about who made whom do what, in connection with the baby, was like past arguments they had described that had happened before Holly became involved with George. Each was blaming the other for something that was really her own doing. Mrs. S. had not needed to look at the baby if she had not wanted to. Holly did not need her mother to decide for her whether she would keep the baby. If she wanted to keep him, the worker would be glad to help her work out plans for taking care of him. But she must be clear in her mind that this was her decision and her responsibility, not her mother's.

The worker pointed out that basically Holly and Mrs. S. needed each other and could have a good relationship. But a relationship built on accusation and manipulation was not healthy for either of them. They both loved the baby, and the main job was to think in terms of what would be best for him. It was time for them to stop accusing each other and to join in considering the baby's welfare.

Holly said she wanted a little more time. Much would depend on what happened when George visited in the next few weeks. She knew she could never take care of the baby, work, and go to school at night, and she would not ask her mother to start raising a child all over again.

Two weeks later Mrs. S. telephoned and asked the worker to see her and Holly. Both were in a panic when they came to the office. George had arrived and had offered to marry Holly if she were willing to join him with the baby. Mrs. S. had fully expected Holly to accept. Although unhappy at the thought, she had realized this would have to be Holly's decision.

Holly, almost inarticulate with distress, begged her mother to talk for her. Mrs. S. urged her to tell her own story. Holly said it was a terrible shock to see George and to size him up after all this time. Maybe she had known all along what he was really like, but she saw him in a totally different light now. "He's no good as a husband, he's no good as a father, he's just no good. I'm ashamed I ever slept with him." Tempting as it was to marry him so she could keep the baby, she was almost sure she was going to tell him No. "The sickening part of it is, I think it won't matter an awful lot to him."

Holly relinquished the baby some three weeks after this interview. She was dejected at losing him, but there were compensations. She was enjoying work and school, her relationship with her mother was vastly improved, and she took great satisfaction in the part she had played in bringing this change about.

The change in Holly's relationship with her mother was evident in the last, and most crucial, decision Holly had to make. Mrs. S. participated as a concerned mother rather than as the willing victim of a manipulative daughter. She was able to stand by and allow Holly to work through her distress to arrive at her own decision, encouraging her to tell her own story to the worker when Holly tried to get her to speak for her. Holly herself was able to arrive at her decision on the basis of essentials;

namely, George's unsuitability as a potential husband and father, rather than in terms of how she could use the situation to control her mother.

It is doubtful whether Holly could have made the progress she did without the changes in Mrs. S. They were so deeply involved with each other that any gains Holly made independently of her mother would have been undone if Mrs. S. had been unable to accept Holly in a new relationship.

Absence of Parental Involvement. Not every parent becomes as involved in her daughter's treatment as Mrs. S. did. Fear of their own emotions, hostility toward the girl, transportation problems and work schedules, separately and in combination, can keep parents from participating in the agency's work with her. In such instances an adolescent can be significantly helped without the active participation of the parents if they are not threatened by her relationship with the worker and if they do not oppose the worker's objectives for the girl. Often improvements in the girl can bring about improvements in their attitudes toward her.

Corinne's was such a situation.

Corinne R., aged fifteen, entered the maternity home when she was seven months pregnant. She had earlier had a stormy experience as a prenatal outpatient when she had refused to submit to a clinic examination. With a good deal of help from physician, nurse, and social worker, she was able to overcome her fears and was at last pleased that she was doing what was expected of her as a prospective mother. She had made friends with several other girls in the waiting room and claimed to be looking forward to seeing them again when she came into residence.

A few hours after Mrs. R. left, Corinne made the first of a series of phone calls in which she begged her mother to take her home. With the worker she spoke of her fear of spending the night in strange surroundings. She had never been away from home before, not even for a single night. Why did her parents have to choose a time like this to send her away?

The worker said she was puzzled at Corinne's feeling this way because it had been her impression that Corinne had decided on her own to come to the maternity home. Was she mistaken? Corinne agreed that it did look as though she had made this decision herself, but what else could she do after hearing her parents say how terrible it was to have her at home, making her jump into bed every time the doorbell rang because they had told neighbors she was ill?

She seemed obsessed with the idea of going home. The only way to keep her would have been by coercion or seduction, either of which would have presented problems. The worker said that apparently the only thing for Corinne to do was to call and tell her mother she wanted to go home. Corinne demurred at first, wanting the worker to call, but finally agreed that it was up to her to do this.

With a good deal of crying Corinne again begged her mother to let her come home. Mrs. R. seemed panic-stricken at the thought of Corinne's coming home, yet was unable to resist her pleas. She asked the worker to "lay down the law" to her. In Corinne's presence the worker explained to Mrs. R. that, although she thought Corinne should stay, she (the worker) did not have the authority to insist. This would have to come from the parents. She offered to talk with them and Corinne again.

When the worker told Corinne she could decide whether she was to stay or leave, Corinne burst into tears. She said she knew she should stay, but something was pulling her home. She spoke of the many mistakes she had made in the past and saw her pregnancy as the culmination of her poor life management. What if going home should turn out to be still another mistake? This time it could be serious.

The worker agreed that this was a difficult decision, but explained that along with the privilege of making one's own decisions went the consequences of sometimes making mistakes. This was one of the features of growing up. Understandably it was frightening to Corinne. Yet she had done well in one difficult situation, the clinic experience, and could probably do well this time also. If Corinne should find that going home was a mistake, there would be time for her to return to the maternity home if she allowed for the six weeks' minimum residence requirement.

Corinne left for home that evening. The following afternoon she telephoned, asking to come back, and be readmitted the next morning.

At this point Corinne was behaving more like a teen-ager than a prospective mother. She seemed to be using her pregnancy primarily to bedevil her parents. Yet she seemed to need, more than anything, an opportunity to make a decision she could consider her own. She felt, probably with some justification, that this chance had been denied her until now. Nevertheless, she was fearful of the responsibility implied in doing what she wished.

Because Corinne was an adolescent, she had to learn by experience; the well-known adolescent propensity for "reality testing." She had to go through the motions of coming into residence of her own volition. But she also had to know there were limits to her decision-making—in this case, the maternity home's minimum residence requirement.

To be sure, there was the risk that Corinne might have decided not to return. But there seemed no alternative. The parents were unable to insist on her staying, and the worker was in no position to do so. Moreover, had Corinne been forced to remain, it would probably have created a massive management problem to keep her in residence. Yet she needed help.

The overriding concern at this point was to try to maintain a contact with her. To have given her an ultimatum, that she would not be permitted to return if she left, would have been to close all doors to possible help. There was a chance that she might return if she could leave without feeling guilty and incompetent. As it turned out, no one was discommoded by her going, except for a minor administrative inconvenience.

When Corinne came to talk with the worker, she was puzzled and embarrassed. She could not understand what had got into her that had made her "practically crazy with the idea of going home." Even while she was insisting on going, she was hoping she would be allowed to return, because she knew she was better off in the maternity home than in her own home.

Could the worker understand? It seemed so terribly important to her to walk out the door and walk in again on her own, not because someone else thought it would be good for her, but because she herself knew it was right. Being home for one night made her realize that they would all be miserable if she were to remain at home for the next two months.

Corinne associated this episode with something that had happened when her parents first learned she was pregnant. They had discussed at some length the pros and cons of an abortion, but they made no attempt to include her in the discussion; they had talked as though she were hardly the person involved. To her, their behavior was the ultimate in rejection—not only that they did not include her in the conversation, but that they would even consider such a thing. She was bursting with fury and shame at the time but could not open her mouth to talk because she felt she had no right to because her pregnancy was causing her parents so much unhappiness. It was as though they were trying to get rid of her now the way they had tried to get rid of the baby before.

She was sorry about all the trouble she had caused, and also ashamed. But maybe it was worth it. In the two days she was home, she and her mother talked to each other the way they never had before, "even about that abortion bit."

Corinne made a good adjustment at the home. She was active in house affairs, handled herself well in relation to other residents, and showed more independence and self-confidence than one would have anticipated from her earlier behavior. She had regular contacts with the worker, using them for the most part to try to clarify her confusing changeability regarding her parents, wanting them to make many decisions for her, yet getting angry when they did so without her consent.

Corinne's infrequent references to the baby were at best indifferent, if not actively hostile. She did not respond to the worker's suggestions that this feeling might change later in the pregnancy or after the baby was born.

She still felt friendly toward the baby's father but was not sure they would continue to see each other after this was over. He was sorry about her being pregnant and seemed concerned about her, but there was not much he could do to help her. He would like to visit her, but she was not sure he would be able to because of the distance, particularly since he worked after school and had no car. The few times Corinne spoke of him it was more as a friend or brother than as a sexual partner or the father of her baby. In some ways one had the impression that this was a pair of young people whose glands had far outdistanced their emotional and social maturity.

The following is a summary of Corinne's experiences in her relationship with her baby. At certain points it resembles Camilla's and may in some ways sound repetitious. It is presented in detail because the way Corinne used this relationship has implications for other adolescent unmarried mothers.

Corinne gave birth to a baby boy after an uneventful delivery. When the worker visited her at the hospital the next day, Corinne was in tears. She said the baby had been brought to her that morning for his first regular feeding, which was contrary to her earlier plan to see him just once through the nursery glass. She did not know how this mistake could have been made. She had a vague recollection that she may have asked for him as soon as she woke up, but she was not sure.

While she was giving him the bottle, he began to choke. In her fright Corinne called the nurse to take him away and told her not to bring him again. Now she had this terrible need to hold him again, to see him and feed him, but she was afraid if she did the choking might recur. She was also afraid she would not be able to relinquish him if she had any further contact with him and grew too fond of him. Corinne clearly was frightened about the meaning of this unexpected turn in her feelings for the baby.

Here was a dependent, immature adolescent whose first attempt to function in an adult role; namely, feeding her baby, had ended in a near disaster. Her first impulse was to deny herself as a mother and to have no further contact with him. This may also have been her way of expressing her hostility toward the child who had forced her to grow up before her time.

She was young to be a mother. Perhaps it would be just as well to let her remain an adolescent and spare her another encounter with the child she thought she had almost killed the first time. But this would have meant that a girl who had seen herself as inept and blundering for much of her life would be adding to these shortcomings the supreme failure of not being able to meet the most elementary requirement of being a mother; namely, giving her baby nurture.

It would have been inappropriate at this point to approach Corinne as an adolescent. Her feelings were much the same as those expressed by other newly delivered mothers who face early, unavoidable, and permanent separation from their babies. She had to be dealt with as a mother who had to make an important decision about her relationship with her baby, rather than as a fractious adolescent. She needed adult support regarding her right to make this decision.

The worker explained that it was natural for Corinne to feel as she did and that it was all right for her to decide whether she wanted to take care of the baby further. The worker then reviewed with Corinne some of the previous crises she had weathered, pointing out how she had grown through them and had been able to make good decisions and to deal with the mistakes also. The worker agreed that handling the baby might make it more difficult to leave him, although this was not inevitable. Not all girls reacted the same way to this experience. For some, taking care of their baby seemed to make the separation easier. The worker admitted that this was the most difficult of the decisions Corinne was likely to make in this experience, but she was confident Corinne could come through it well, whichever way she decided.

The worker suggested that if Corinne skipped the next feeding, she might be able to get over this feeling. If, however, she still wanted to have the baby with her after that, she should be guided by her own feelings and should allow herself to enjoy her association with him. The worker thought Corinne need not worry about the possibility of the baby's choking on his food. This often happens with new babies, and many mothers become terrified at it, whether they are younger or older, married or not. A nurse could be with Corinne during the next feeding if she liked.

Corinne decided later that day to have the baby with her for the rest of the hospital stay. The nurse later reported that she handled him lovingly and comfortably and seemed to have a happy time with him.

The final separation was difficult. Corinne told the worker she cried when she left the baby, and for a moment almost regretted having allowed herself to become so attached to him. Then she remembered how proud she was each time they brought him to her and how good it felt to hold him. She wished her mother could have seen the way she handled him, but the hospital did not allow visitors during feeding time. She was pleased that she had not gone to pieces when she gave him up. One thing that made it easier was seeing him go with someone she liked, the worker from the children's agency.

Because Mrs. R. had remained uninvolved, the worker had taken a mothering role toward Corinne in order to give her the support she needed to carry out her own maternal function toward her baby. However, the worker kept the parents informed about her work with Corinne and was careful not to pre-empt their authority in matters that were theirs to decide. The parents were pleased with Corinne's adjustment in the home and with her more mature approach. They were particularly impressed with the self-confidence and reasonableness with which she talked about the baby.

Health Care

Adolescents, married or unmarried, are considered high obstetric risks.[2] They and their babies are considered more vulnerable than others to the effects of toxemia, to premature birth and its attendant anomalies, and to maternal and perinatal accidents. It is generally agreed that many of these hazards can be reduced through early and regular prenatal care.

Yet many unmarried pregnant teen-agers do not receive the care they should have. Often they are deterred by the same factors that affect older women: [3] ineligibility because of non-residency; failure to prove medical indigency, coupled with inability to pay; applying too late in the pregnancy; and unpleasant clinic conditions—tedious questioning about eligibility, long waits in crowded, depressing surroundings, cursory handling, seeing a different (sometimes an indifferent) doctor each time, transportation problems, and the like. The wish to conceal the pregnancy can also be a compelling deterrent to a teen-ager.

The requirement that she bring parental consent can keep a teen-ager from obtaining prenatal care. Recognizing that this simply increases the hazard, some clinics have begun to relax this requirement. A national organization "advocate[s] legislation permitting the provision of medical care by a physician without parental knowledge or consent to pregnant minors and to minor parents when, in the physician's judgment, the absence of such care may jeopardize the health of the minor." [4] As one obstetrician observed, "It's a lot more important to get a girl into prenatal care and to keep her there than it is to risk losing her by insisting on her mother's written consent before we'll do anything."

Teen-agers are particularly sensitive to the way they are dealt with by clinic personnel. Added to other discomforts, many of them are afraid and embarrassed about the pelvic examination. They need understanding and reassurance at such a time. They need to know what is going to happen and why certain procedures are necessary. They need to be handled with tact and sensitivity. To assume that their sexual activity has rendered them impervious to shame is to underestimate the naïveté, even the prudishness, of many pregnant adolescents. If their encounters with clinic staff are humiliating, they are not likely to return. Witness the experience of one fifteen-year-old:

After a two-hour wait in a crowded clinic she is ushered into an examining cubicle that is separated from the waiting room by a curtain through which she has already heard discomforting sounds as previous patients were examined. She is examined by one doctor, with two others ("awfully young ones") in attendance. During the examination she is asked how long she has been having sexual relations. She does not reply, but hears the examining doctor remark to the others on the young age at which girls become sexually active these days. After she leaves, she refuses to return to this clinic—or to any other.

In the last decade there has been a growing effort to bring more pregnant teen-agers, especially unmarried ones, into early and continuous prenatal care. Some clinics have made a special effort to make the physical surroundings attractive to pregnant teen-agers (and to other pregnant women as well) and to reduce waiting time by working on an appointment schedule, or by setting aside special clinic hours for them. Transportation problems are reduced through the use of such facilities as neighborhood clinics and maternal and infant care centers. In rural areas traveling "clinicmobiles" are used, or special arrangements are made to bring patients to the clinic.

Some health programs for teen-age unmarried mothers are linked to special educational programs.[5] These, too, are usually structured to encourage pregnant teen-agers to seek early prenatal care and to stay with it. In many programs the girl sees the same doctor at each visit and, wherever possible, is also delivered by him.

According to reports from many of these programs, reducing deterrents does bring teen-agers into prenatal care and, what is more important, keeps them in care throughout the pregnancy. Attendance at the clinic is uniformly reported to be high, often exceeding initial expectations. Correspondingly, maternal and fetal hazards for this high-risk group are thought to have been reduced, one program reporting that a group of teen-agers was transformed from high to normal risk.[6]

Another important health problem is the question of nutrition for the pregnant teen-ager. As a prospective mother she should follow a diet that provides adequate nutrition for her and her baby and that minimizes the risks of excessive weight gain, fluid retention, edema, elevated blood pressure, and so forth. Often this means giving up favorite foods that are part of the standard teen-age diet: soda pop, hot dogs, potato chips, pizza, and candy bars. This is no easy task for a teen-ager, pregnant or not.

Many adolescents are reasonably faithful to their diets. Others have difficulty. They may deliberately flout dietary requirements as a way of defying what they consider to be unnecessary controls imposed by overanxious and restrictive adults. Others may turn to their favorite foods for comfort in time of anxiety.

If a teen-ager's eating habits result in undesirable medical consequences, the problem has to be dealt with in terms of the emotional condition that causes her to disregard her and her baby's health this way. Sometimes the opportunity to express her dissatisfaction or her anxiety (often in relation to an entirely different question) can be enough to help her accept the necessary restrictions.

Some physicians have begun to question whether *a priori* dietary restrictions, not related to a specific medical condition, need to be as limiting as they sometimes are. Some wonder whether the tensions generated are worth the effort of trying to enforce a strict regimen.

The United States Department of Agriculture notes in connection with a grant to the University of Vermont for a four-year study of "The Influence of Diet on the Course of Teen-age Pregnancy": "The government wants to find out what pregnant teenagers should eat. . . . Scientists already know that complicated pregnancies occur more often in adolescents than in adults, but they don't know whether to blame it on poor nutrition." [7]

To some teen-agers, simply being confronted with a series of prohibitions is a signal for them to find ways of circumventing the rules. Often, what and how much a pregnant teen-ager should eat becomes a major issue between her and those responsible for her well-being. Many workers in maternity homes are familiar with the silent battle that is sometimes waged between staff and ingenious teen-agers who manage to find ways of smuggling forbidden snacks into their rooms, there to attract ants and mice and, presumably, to endanger their health.

When diet restrictions are necessary, an adolescent can often respond if the adults are willing to acknowledge her food preferences and to allow her to participate in setting up some of the restrictions. Adolescents can come up with remarkably creative ideas when given an opportunity to put their ingenuity to use in combining good nutrition with fun eating.

Regardless of the debate about the number of candy bars and potato chips a pregnant teen-ager should be allowed, many unmarried mothers whose babies we are trying to save through better prenatal care are financially unable to meet minimum nutritional requirements. Although special instruction in stretching the food dollar may result in improved use of limited funds, one cannot expect to produce an adequate diet from inadequate funds. As one mother of a pregnant teen-ager put it: "Sure, I can fill a meat loaf with bread as good as the next one, but then she's getting starch not meat. You can stretch a dollar just so much, and then it busts. Then you've really got nothing."

Some teen-agers come to the prenatal clinic already damaged by a lifetime of poor nutrition, with irreversible body conditions. Perhaps it is too late to start prenatal care at the prenatal clinic. Perhaps it should have started with the prenatal care of the present mother's mother. In other words, while trying to mitigate the effects of poor life hygiene for the currently pregnant teen-ager, it is important to begin to look to the future for the baby she is bearing.

Many people feel that the most effective way of eliminating the hazards of teen-age unmarried pregnancy is to prevent the pregnancy itself. Since one of the surer preventive measures is the dissemination of birth control information and devices, some maternity clinics offer contraceptive advice and service as part of the six-week postpartum health follow-up to teen-agers who have been in their care.[8] (One clinic is testing the feasibility of preventing a first pregnancy by offering such services to "a selected group of sexually active, nulliparous adolescent girls" as part of a total adolescent program in medical and social care.)[9]

Many people object to birth control programs for adolescents on the grounds that providing them with information on contraception gives tacit encouragement to further sexual activity. For some people birth control is an affront to their religious and moral sensibilities, more abhorrent perhaps than the sexual activity itself. Others feel that such programs are directed primarily toward the Negro and are therefore an indirect attempt at genocide.

Admittedly birth control for teen-agers is a difficult subject. It involves many questions—moral, religious, social, psychological, medical, and legal. Feelings often run high when it is discussed, and it can generate a good deal of conflict within a profession, interprofessionally and in the community at large. In the face of these understandable objections, one can only ask, "What are the alternatives?"

We do not know that withholding birth control information deters a girl from further sexual activity or that giving her such information actually promotes it. We do know, however, that the girl who first becomes pregnant when she is a teen-ager is likely to have additional out-of-wedlock pregnancies.[10] The girls and their babies need to be protected from the risks this entails.

The question of allowing growing numbers of babies to be conceived, to start life with the odds against them, also raises moral, religious, social, psychological, and health questions. There is a growing conviction among many who work with pregnant unmarried teen-agers that the question soon will be not whether they should have birth control service but, rather, how to provide it intelligently and sensitively to those who need it.

This question applies not only to those who are served in free or low-cost clinics, but to those who can pay for it as well. No doubt some adolescents do receive contraceptive advice from private physicians. It is not known how widespread this practice is because, as with many other disapproved social practices, those who can pay for the services do not receive the public attention that is directed toward those who cannot.

Schooling

Continued schooling is a basic need for the unmarried pregnant adolescent. It can provide social and emotional supports for her during the long months of pregnancy. Continuing with a familiar activity can lend a sense of stability in one area of her life when much else is fraught with change. It allows her to have companionship and shared experiences with others of her age. Insofar as a community's investment in education reflects its regard for those it educates, this evidence of the community's concern for her can meliorate some of the opprobrium that in other ways attaches to her condition. It can restore some of her own self-esteem.

In our culture high-school education is the major avenue through which an adolescent begins to prepare for adult career goals and economic self-dependence. More and more, high-school graduation, or its equivalent in training, is becoming the minimum requirement for all sorts of jobs. For the girl who will be keeping her baby, economic self-dependence can be an important goal.

Some girls can continue their education as residents of maternity homes. Others receive home instruction under "handicapped child" programs. A few school systems allow them to attend night school. These arrangements take care of a small proportion of the adolescent unmarried mother population.

For the vast majority of schoolgirls, however, pregnancy signals the end of their schooling. Usually a girl is expelled from school as soon as it is known she is pregnant. In most instances she is not permitted to return. Reports from forty-two school systems that set up special programs for pregnant school girls indicate: "About two-thirds of the school systems in areas served by the programs insist girls leave school immediately upon discovering their pregnancies. . . . Twenty of the school systems . . . allow the girls to return to the same school following delivery." [11]

In addition to the girls who are not permitted to return, there are the ones who are discouraged about returning because they have been expelled and have lost contact with the school community. Some cannot go back because they must take care of their babies. In Maryland, for instance, pregnancy is the most frequent single condition causing an adolescent to leave school prior to graduation. More than twice as many girls leave for this reason as for all other physical and medical reasons.[12]

The number of teen-aged unmarried mothers is likely to increase as the number of teen-agers increases. It is estimated that in 1966 approximately 72,000 schoolgirls gave birth to out-of-wedlock babies [13] and that in the five years prior to 1965 the average increase was about 4,000 each year.[14] If this trend continues, it means that we are rapidly producing in this country a sizable and permanent population of school dropouts who, with their children, are likely to be caught in the social and economic vise this lack of education often creates.

In a growing number of communities programs have been developed, with new ones constantly being added, for the continued education of schoolgirl unmarried mothers.[15] These programs are broadly based so far as organization, sponsorship, and funding are concerned. Since most of them are required to hold classes away from the regular school buildings, they have often had to resort to makeshifts. Storefronts, churches, renovated residences, and even mobile classrooms have been used. As of this writing only the more fortunate projects—of which there are but a few—have their own buildings. In most instances education is part of a larger program that usually includes health and social welfare services.[16]

The common concern is to keep the pregnant schoolgirl related to an educational program in the hope that she will be able to complete high school or resume her regular schooling after the baby is born. Some educators see this as an opportunity to improve the attitudes of girls who have been discouraged about learning and about themselves through previous experiences in overcrowded, dilapidated, and poorly equipped ghetto schools. Small classes, conducted in a warm and accepting climate, a variety of academic, vocational, and practical subjects taught by teachers who are committed to the idea that everyone is capable of learning something, are considered the prerequisites for a receptive learning situation. It is thought that a successful learning experience, which in addition to the usual school subjects, includes learning about her body, her pregnancy, and her coming child, can not only better prepare a girl for her life tasks but can also give her an improved sense of her worth as a person and as a female.

Those who have reported the results of their programs are uniformly pleased with the educational performance of a majority of their pupils.[17] They report that most girls attend school conscientiously and maintain or improve their grades. Some girls, who would otherwise have left school, were encouraged to continue to graduation. A few have gone on to college or have taken specialized postgraduate training.

But these programs can accommodate only a small percentage

of unmarried mothers, currently estimated at 8,000 per year.[18] No doubt there will be room for more as the number of programs increases. There is serious question, however, whether communities can or will ever undertake the cost of special education for all unmarried mothers who should have it.

Some communities, anticipating this problem, permit pregnant schoolgirls to continue in their regular school programs if they wish. Atlanta, the first to allow them to do so, has been followed by New York City. No doubt other cities will be joining them. One of the advantages of this approach is that it removes the education of the pregnant schoolgirl from the realm of special privilege, where, in effect, it now is, and endows it with the authority of public responsibility. Another advantage is that it enables any pregnant girl who wishes to do so to continue her education. In any event, the decision to remain in her regular program should be arrived at jointly by the girl, her parents, her doctor, and the appropriate school personnel, and should be based on her physical and emotional status as well as on the social climate of the school community.

Some people fear that the presence of a pregnant girl in the classroom may act as a contaminant, so to speak, that may encourage illegitimacy among some of her more susceptible classmates. We have no data to indicate whether this is so or not. It can probably be argued the other way also—that is, that seeing a pregnant girl day after day may act as a deterrent to others. To quote from a report mentioned earlier:

Most young girls want to be attractive and active. The result of a relationship leading to pregnancy is that a girl becomes heavy, unwieldly and—for a time—less attractive than one who is not pregnant. She cannot dance or play volleyball. She may be lonely and frightened and troubled. To see a classmate paying this penalty, and see visible evidence that she is about to be burdened with the responsibility which is bound to conflict with fun, could have a more sobering effect on students than any number of lectures by adults who are regarded as stodgy, mealy-mouthed and alien. All in all it is conceivable that allowing pregnant girls to stay in school would discourage more illegitimacy than it would promote.[19]

More important than the possibility of contagion are the educational questions that occur in connection with a pregnant girl's staying in her regular school program. She is, after all, as much a pregnant girl as she is a schoolgirl. Pregnancy affects her physically and psychologically. We do not have much information about the effects of pregnancy on mental processes, but it is conceivable that body chemistry and other physiological changes may affect learning. We know that for many women, particularly in the late stages, part of being pregnant means being passive, slower paced and lethargic. Moreover, many of these girls have worries. Those who expect to keep their babies may wonder how they can accommodate their education and career goals to early motherhood and family responsibility. Those who expect to surrender their babies may wonder how difficult it will be to separate from them. In other respects, also, they are subject to the same crises as are adult unmarried mothers.

Can one expect an unmarried pregnant schoolgirl to follow a consistent learning pattern throughout her pregnancy? Should programming and scheduling take into account the possibility that her capacity to learn may be influenced by the stage of pregnancy or the stresses she is undergoing at a given time? Can she be expected to do better on exams at certain points than at others? Can she learn better from books at one point, from pictures, concrete objects, or activity at another? How can curriculum, syllabus, and method be adapted to the fact that the pupil is pregnant and sometimes in distress? Above all, how can these differences, if they are differences, be provided for in a regular school program that is geared to nonpregnant adolescents?

If we are to educate large numbers of pregnant schoolgirls, school programs will have to be tailored to the conditions that affect the way they learn. It is important that the school program not assume disproportionate prominence in relation to other aspects of the unmarried pregnant teen-ager's circumstances. Because schoolwork is an approved activity, it can be used by the girl (and frequently by her parents also) to avoid one of the important tasks of her experience; namely, coming to terms with her image of herself as a mother and her responsibility to her baby. In our enthusiasm for education we may be tempted to give priority to her school activity, emphasizing the schoolgirl role at the expense of the maternal role. The experience with Nellie is a case in point.

Nellie, aged sixteen, was a bright girl, full of adolescent mischief at times, yet a constructive leader in the maternity home. She was devoted to her high-school studies and carried a five-subject schedule without difficulty. She was always busy, planning social affairs, handling house government problems, and studying. She had little time for questions that implied a baby was coming, about which she might be having some feelings.

Much of her contact with the social worker centered around planning subjects for the following semester, college entrance requirements, and the like. There was an occasional stab, and a hasty retreat when questions about possible reactions to the birth of the baby, feelings about involvement of the baby's father, and similar subjects were raised.

A few weeks before her baby was due, the baby's father telephoned to ask Nellie whether he could visit her and the baby at the hospital. (She had not seen him since entering the maternity home.) His request came as a surprise, and it upset her. She had thought she had little feeling for him, and now everything was all stirred up again. For the first time she talked meaningfully about her feelings for the baby's father and about her growing and troubling feelings for the baby.

At about this time she began to complain about not being able to concentrate on her schoolwork and decided to drop two of the five exams for which she had been preparing. "Is there something wrong with me?" she asked. "All of a sudden this stuff doesn't mean a thing to me. I'll be lucky if I can get through the three subjects. It seems all I want to do the next few weeks is just sit around and be pregnant."

When Nellie informed a dismayed staff of her decision, they tried to convince her of the folly of risking a semester's credit for the sake of two courses. When she insisted, they surmised that she was either on the verge of a depression or that long-controlled hostility toward authority was probably at the bottom of her reaction.

For a long time Nellie had used her approved role as an adolescent schoolgirl and house leader to suppress her tasks as a prospective mother. However, her commitment to her teen-age activities weakened when the telephone call from the baby's father forced her to face her feelings about him and her baby. It would have been unfortunate if adult disapproval of her changed feeling had caused her to feel that school achievement was more important than "just being pregnant" and that her decision to accept herself in a maternal role was inappropriate.

The regular school is in a strategic position to help the pregnant adolescent. School is where a teen-ager spends most of her time and where, aside from her home, she is likely to have the most meaningful relationships. Her mood and behavior in the classroom may, to a sensitive teacher, be the first signs of distress. Through the nurse or school social worker, she can be referred to an appropriate agency for help. A girl is more likely to turn to the school for help if she perceives it as a helping agent. If, however, she thinks she will be expelled if her condition is found out, she is likely to postpone letting anyone know and, as was noted earlier, may delay obtaining much-needed prenatal care.

Increasingly schools are taking a realistic position with regard to pregnancy among their students and are permitting them to return without penalty.[20] Trying to protect the other students from knowing about their classmate's situation is often futile. Most are apt to be aware of the facts when a classmate leaves because she is pregnant, regardless of official explanations. In discussions with adolescent unmarried mothers in a maternity home, it was noted:

They . . . surmised that many of their schoolmates were aware of the facts or had strong suspicions. . . . Certain explanations for leaves of absence from school were, in the words of some, "dead give-aways." Mononucleosis, nervous exhaustion, a suddenly-decided-upon extended visit to a distant aunt, a term at boarding school—these and other explanations have apparently become the germ of a vocabulary which, when employed by some of our young people under certain conditions, take on rather specific meaning.[21]

School is often an important factor in the adjustment of the girl who has had her baby. It is the major channel through which she can take up her career tasks. It provides contacts with contemporaries and specific objectives at a time when she may be trying to find a balance between her recent sobering experiences and the sometimes mindless high jinks of adolescence, which, at this moment, she may see as mere "kid stuff" as she wonders what she ever saw in those activities before she became pregnant. If her classmates have not been prejudiced by their elders, most of them are likely to accept her back, a few perhaps with the unspoken thought, "There, but for the grace of God. . . ."

The Young Mother

The adolescent unmarried mother who keeps her child has to reconcile the continuing demands of her responsibilities as a mother with her needs as an adolescent. It is a difficult task. Her needs as an adolescent may suffer because often she finds herself in a social limbo. It is difficult to accommodate a baby's schedule to the spontaneous activity that constitutes so much of adolescent social life. The novelty of the baby may attract her friends for a time. But when the novelty has worn off, she may find that she and her childless contemporaries have less and less in common to talk about. Contacts become fewer, until finally she is without suitable companionship. If she is unable to arrange for the care of the baby, she may have to drop out of school, becoming further removed from contact with her contemporaries. The potentially harmful effects of such isolation on the unmarried mother and on her attitude toward her baby need hardly be spelled out.

Some agencies—group service agencies, health agencies, maternity homes, and casework agencies, to name only a few—have undertaken to provide for the postpartum social and recreational needs of adolescent unmarried mothers who have responsibility for the care of their babies. Many of the programs provide baby-sitting service for when the girl is taking part in the program. A number of comprehensive care programs have added to their services full-time mother and baby day-care centers in which schooling and child care can be provided simultaneously under the same roof for the teen-age unmarried mother who wishes to continue her education. While the mother attends school, the child is taken care of in the nursery. After school, under adult guidance and support, the young mother is taught how to take care of her baby and, it is hoped, learns to enjoy him.[22]

A number of agencies report that group discussions about child care and the special problems connected with being a young unmarried mother often led to discussions of problems girls were having with their parents, particularly their mothers. When the girls' mothers were invited to participate in some of the discussions, several mothers and daughters were able to resolve their conflicts with each other—conflicts that had arisen because the girl's mother wanted to pre-empt the relationship with the baby or because the girl was using him to settle old scores with her mother.

Some young unmarried mothers—many of them no more than sixteen years old—establish themselves independently in the community with their babies. Many suffer severe economic hardships, living in dilapidated, unsanitary quarters, sometimes in disorganized communal arrangements. They have a hard time managing the care of their babies and the tasks of house-keeping. Health problems are not uncommon among them.

In many instances, the problems that have kept them from returning to their families have also left them poorly equipped to cope with the tasks they have taken on. Often the mothers are themselves as much in need of nurture as are the babies to whom they are supposed to give it. The unmarried mother may need a relationship with a mother-person who, while helping her to learn responsible motherhood, can at the same time allow her to satisfy some of her own unmet dependency needs.

Some adolescents can probably benefit from the type of half-way house described earlier. Others may need more help and closer relationships than the halfway house can provide. They may need a small group home, individual foster family care, or some form of extended maternity home care in which they can be with people with him they already have a relationship. Such arrangements, besides meeting the practical and emotional needs of the adolescent unmarried mother, can also provide a living experience in taking care of a child. When she later establishes herself independently with her baby, she can do so with confidence, knowing she has demonstrated her competence as a mother. The girl whose plan to keep the baby is practically and emotionally unsound can use the experience to reassess her plan without exposing the baby to the hazards of inadequate care.

NOTES

1. The point of view presented in this chapter was first stated by the writer in "Perspectives on Services for Teenage Unmarried Mothers," *Child Welfare* 43 (January 1964), pp. 5–13. See also Maurine LaBarre, "The Triple Crisis: Adolescence, Early Marriage, and Parenthood. Part I—Motherhood," *The Double Jeopardy, The Triple Crisis: Illegitimacy Today* (New York: National Council on Illegitimacy, 1969), pp. 9–21.

2. For studies of teen-age pregnancy, see Frederick C. Battaglia, Todd M. Frazier, and Andre E. Hellegers, "Obstetric and Pediatric Complications of Juvenile Pregnancy," *Pediatrics* 32 (November 1963), pp. 902–10; Richard M. Briggs, Reginald R. Herren, and William Benbow Thompson, Sr., "Pregnancy in the Young Adolescent," *American Journal of Obstetrics and Gynecology* (August 1962), pp. 436–41; Leon S. Israel and J. D. Deutschberger, "Relation of Mother's Age to Obstetric Performance," *Obstetrics and Gynecology* 24 (September 1964), pp. 411–17; Thomas J. Mussio, "Primigravidas Under Age 14," *American Journal of Obstetrics and Gynecology* 84 (August 1962), pp. 442–44; Jean Pakter, et. al., "Out-of-Wedlock Births in New York City: II—Medical Aspects," *American Journal of Public Health* 51 (June 1961), pp. 846–65; Philip M. Sarrel, "The University Hospital and the Teenage Unwed Mother," *American Journal of Public Health* 57 (August 1967), pp. 1308–13; J. P. Semmens, "Implications of Teenage Pregnancy," *Obstetrics and Gynecology* 26 (July 1965), pp. 77–84; and

Howard J. Osofsky, *The Pregnant Teenager* (Springfield, Ill.: Charles C Thomas, 1968); Ross Roundtable on Maternal and Child Nursing No. 2, *The Adolescent Unmarried Mother*, Columbus, Ohio: Ross Laboratories, 1965; and James P. Semmens and William Lamers, Jr., *Teen-age Pregnancy* (Springfield, Ill.: Charles C Thomas, 1968).

Many of the factors regarding availability and use of health services for adolescents apply to older unmarried mothers as well, particularly those who cannot afford private care. For more general discussions of this problem, and corrective programs, see Blanche Bernstein and Mignon Sauber, *Deterrents to Early Prenatal Care and Social Services Among Women Pregnant Out-of-Wedlock* (Albany: New York State Department of Social Welfare, 1960), a study conducted under the auspices of the Community Council of Greater New York; Edwin M. Gold, "A Broad View of Maternity Care," *Children* 9 (March-April 1962), pp. 52–58; U.S. Department of Health, Education, and Welfare, *Health Services for Unmarried Mothers*, prepared for the Children's Bureau by Elizabeth Herzog and Rose Bernstein (Washington, D.C.: Government Printing Office, 1964); Virginia Insley, "Some Implications of Recent Legislation for Social Work," in *Mothers-at-Risk*, ed. Florence Haselkorn (Garden City, N.Y.: Adelphi University School of Social Work, 1966), pp. 48–59; Arthur J. Lesser, "High Risk Mothers and Infants: Problems and Prospects for Prevention," in Haselkorn, *Mothers-at-Risk*, pp. 15–25; and Howard B. Monahan and Esther G. Spencer, "Deterrents to Prenatal Care," *Children* 9 (May-June 1962), pp. 114–19.

3. Bernstein and Sauber, *Deterrents to Early Prenatal Care*. Also Howard B. Monahan and Esther C. Spencer, "Deterrents to Prenatal Care," *Children* 9 (May-June 1962), pp. 114–19.

4. *NCI* (National Council on Illegitimacy) *Newsletter* 9 (Spring 1969), p. 3.

5. These programs are discussed more fully in the section on schooling. For a discussion of programs to bring more pregnant women of any age into prenatal care, see Edwin M. Gold, "A Broad View of Maternity Care," *Children* 9 (March-April 1962), pp. 52–58.

6. C. George Murdock, "The Unmarried Mother and the School

System," *American Journal of Public Health* 58 (December 1968), pp. 2217–24.

7. The Miami *Herald,* September 14, 1969. See also *A Positive Approach to Unmarried Mothers,* Fourth Progress Report (Philadelphia: Berean Parental-Vocational-Educational Program, 1963). Since the book went to press, these questions have been underscored in *Maternal Nutrition and the Course of Pregnancy,* the report of a study conducted under the auspices of the National Research Council. As reported in part in the Boston *Globe,* Thursday, July 30, 1970, "The committee found no evidence that excessive weight gain causes toxemia." Quoting from the study, "Diets and dietary regimens commonly used in pre-natal clinics are not suitable for adolescents. The diet of a young pregnant girl especially must be individualized."

8. Sarrel, "The University Hospital."

9. Leon Gordis, et. al., "Adolescent Pregnancy: A Hospital-Based Program for Primary Prevention," *American Journal of Public Health* 58 (May 1968), p. 849.

10. Philip M. Sarrel and Clarence D. Davis, "The Young Unwed Primipara," *American Journal of Obstetrics and Gynecology* 95 (July 1966), pp. 722–25.

11. U.S. Department of Health, Education, and Welfare, *Multi-service Programs for Pregnant School Girls,* prepared for the Children's Bureau by Marian Howard (Washington, D.C.: Government Printing Office, 1968), p. 4.

12. Oscar D. Stine, Rowland V. Rider, and Eileen Sweeney, "School Leaving Due to Pregnancy in an Urban Adolescent Population," *American Journal of Public Health* 54 (January 1964), pp. 1–6.

13. U.S. Department of Health, Education, and Welfare, *Vital Statistics of the United States,* Vol. 1 (Washington, D.C.: Government Printing Office, 1968).

14. *Trends in Illegitimacy, United States, 1940–65* (Washington, D.C.: Government Printing Office, 1968).

15. Some programs include teen-age married mothers also.

16. For an overview of the varied programs, see Howard, *Multi-service Programs,* pp. 2–3; and Marian Howard, "Comprehensive Service Programs for School-Age Pregnant Girls," *Children* 15 (September-October 1968), pp. 193–97. The picture is changing so rapidly that, as of this writing, both these reviews are based on what by now must be only a small proportion of

existing programs. More recent information can be obtained from the National Council on Illegitimacy, New York City, and from Dr. Charles P. Gershenson, Director of Research, Children's Bureau, U.S. Department of Health, Education, and Welfare, Washington, D.C.

17. So many of these programs have been reported, both in the professional journals and in the press, that it would be arbitrary to single out any one. One report is referred to, however, because it deals with several aspects of the program, from its inception through its incorporation into an on-going community system. See U.S. Department of Health, Education, and Welfare, *The Webster School: A District of Columbia Program for Pregnant Girls*, Children's Bureau Research Reports, No. 2, prepared for the Children's Bureau by Marion Howard (Washington, D.C.: Government Printing Office, 1968).

18. Howard, "Comprehensive Service Programs."

19. Herzog and Bernstein, *Health Services for Unmarried Mothers*, p. 48.

20. Robert L. Noland and Catherine Sherry, "Educator Attitudes and Practices Regarding the Pregnant High School Girl," *Mental Hygiene* 51 (January 1967), pp. 49–54.

21. Bernstein, "One Hundred Unmarried Mothers and Their Problems," unpublished study (Boston: Crittenton Hastings House, 1961–63).

22. One of the oldest of these programs is the Berean Parental-Vocational-Educational Program in Philadelphia.

6

THE UNMARRIED FATHER

It has long been recognized that agencies serving unmarried mothers have not given enough attention to unmarried fathers. In 1918 it was noted that "by far the weakest part of the case work done in regard to the problem of the unmarried mother is that relating to the father." [1] In 1940 the subject received major attention at the National Conference of Social Work, at which time it was stressed that, although agencies acknowledged the importance of knowing more about unmarried fathers, little was being done to obtain the necessary information about them.[2] Yet, until some fifteen years ago, agency services and public interest centered, for the most part, on the unmarried mother and her baby, as though unmarried parenthood were a unilateral affair.[3]

The situation has been changing of late. Agencies that traditionally limited their contacts to the unmarried mother have increasingly been reaching out to the unmarried father as well. They are interested in him not only in terms of his responsibility to the mother and child, but also because they want to understand him as a person with needs and rights of his own. They want to know him better so they can approach him more intelligently.

Some of the questions about unmarried fathers to which answers are sought are: Do unmarried fathers have special characteristics or needs that predispose them to unwed parenthood? What is an appropriate role for an agency in relation to an unmarried father? How can an agency involve him in its planning for the mother and the child?

The following discussion is based on studies and practitioner opinions, including a few of my own.[4] The applicability of the findings and conclusions is limited. Besides the limitations described in the footnote, the information given by the unmarried parents must also be interpreted in terms of their bias. Unmarried parenthood involves a highly sensitive aspect of human experience, one that not many people are given to discussing frankly with strangers. Moreover, the unmarried parents' contact with the agency relates to events that, since they took place, have become tinged with censure and social hazard, possibly with a threat of legal involvement for the man.

Under the circumstances it is understandable that an unmarried father would want to put his best foot forward in talking with a representative of a community agency about his relationship with the unmarried mother. The unmarried mother, on her part, may interpret events according to the image of herself she is trying to preserve, or by the pressures of the moment, particularly as they involve the unmarried father's behavior toward her at a given time.

The discussion must therefore be interpreted with these limitations in mind. Nevertheless, even limited or negative information can be useful. Insofar as it points up gaps in our knowledge and reveals the weak places in our favorite theories, it can furnish the basis for a more studied approach to the use of helping resources.

Predisposing Factors?

A recurring question regarding unmarried fathers is: Is there a relationship between a man's general emotional adjustment and his penchant for illicit fatherhood? Some say there is, that unmarried fatherhood, like unmarried motherhood, is symptomatic. According to this point of view, the unmarried father is seen as the psychological counterpart of his sexual partner, who is herself, presumably, emotionally disturbed; he is "sick by association" and impelled toward unwed paternity by conflicts that parallel hers: uncertainty about his masculinity and fears about latent homosexuality, hostility toward women, rebellion against authority, and the like.

For the most part, evidence to support this point of view is open to the same doubts that pertain to the theory that unmarried women become pregnant because they are emotionally disturbed. As Elizabeth Herzog points out:

According to our reading of *presumptive* evidence, which is the only kind we have on this point, it is not true that to become an unmarried father is an unfailing symptom of psychopathology, calling for therapy. On the contrary, there is enough evidence about unmarried mothers to rule out the blanket assumption that pregnancy out of wedlock inevitably or even usually indicates pathology on the part of the unmarried mother, and there seems no reason to assume more pathology on the part of the unmarried father.[5]

If an unmarried father seems upset when seen at an agency, it may be that he is reacting as much to the realities of his situation as he is to chronic emotional disturbance and, in fact, may be manifesting a healthy awareness of the implications of his circumstances. He may be worried about the threat of a possible court action and resultant financial involvement. He may be concerned about the hazards to his schooling or to his occupational or social standing. He may be worried about possible harm to his wife and children, should his situation become known. He may be genuinely distressed at the plight of the unmarried mother and concerned about the future of his coming child. Or he may indeed be struggling with chronic problems that have been activated or intensified by his unwed parenthood. Prepregnancy personality tests of adolescent boys indicate:

. . . there is very little . . . to support the rather broad and sweeping statements which have been made about out-of-wedlock fathers. Some of these statements may derive from the fact that out-of-wedlock fathers are usually assessed *after* the unfortunate state of affairs has occurred. It is not surprising that the father would show anxiety or depression or fear or various conflicts under these conditions. To say on such evidence, however, that these psychological states have contributed to the out-of-wedlock conception is a little bit like claiming that a study of a group of patients whose appendixes had been removed showed that the cause of their appendicitis was an abdominal scar.[6]

According to several studies, the relationship between the unmarried parents before the women became pregnant had many of the commonly accepted attributes of ordinary male-female relationships. The majority met and associated in a quite respectable context. Over three-fifths of one group of unmarried mothers and fathers met through friends or relatives.[7] In another group, "Most mothers had partners from their home towns, known by their friends and families, and members of peer groups." [8] In still another group, slightly more than half of the unmarried fathers had been known to the girls' parents. Most of these parents spoke of the boys much as parents would of any young men they were evaluating as companions for their daughters. Typical of some of the comments were: "He's all right for a friend, but she can do better for a husband" . . . "We like him all right, but she should have been going out with others besides him" . . . and "We were all intrigued with him. I can see how she would find him different; she's led such a sheltered life. I guess he turned out to be a little too different." [9] Most of the unmarried parents had known each other for periods ranging from several months to more than two years before the woman became pregnant.[10] Fewer than 10 per cent of the pregnancies resulted from a casual association or a pickup.

The studies were also in agreement that the vast majority of unmarried parents were appropriately matched as to age, education, and socio-economic backgrounds—the same conditions that are found among married pairs.[11] In other words, findings from these studies do not support the traditional concept of the unmarried mother as the hapless dupe of a sophisticated seducer, although this is not to deny that in some instances she has been so.

The idea of the male as exploiter of the female was challenged more than a half century ago:

There is an opinion among many people that the unmarried mother is ordinarily a young girl who has been seduced by some man usually considerably her senior. . . . Such a belief cannot be upheld by the results of this study. . . .

These figures, far from emphasizing the element of seduction of young girls by older men, point towards what one might naturally believe; namely, that the discrepancy in age between the unmarried mother and the father of her child conforms to the laws of sexual attraction. The preponderant group of the parents of illegitimate children conceive these children at an age when they were biologically most productive, and sexually most attractive to each other.[12]

Unmarried mothers themselves are often the first to admit to the voluntary nature of their participation in the relationship. True, a girl may be disappointed and bitter at the father's failure to stand by what she thought were assurances of love and protection were she to "get caught," but she does not often present herself as the innocent victim of a wily villain. Fanciful stories to explain the pregnancy—stories of mysterious amnesias, of spiked drinks and forced participation, of having been fed a tainted candy bar, and the like—are considerably less frequent nowadays than they were in the past. "It takes two to tango" is the whimsical euphemism by which the dual involvement is often acknowledged.

At least half of the unmarried mothers in the studies said that their relationships with the unmarried fathers before they became pregnant were those of love or close friendship.[13] The relationships were variously described as "going steady" (by adolescents), "a very deep friendship," "a serious love affair," and "almost engaged." Approximately one-third of the women said that there had been plans for marriage or that the father had promised marriage should a pregnancy occur.

An unusually frank group of women stated that, although they considered the unmarried fathers good friends, they knew the relationship meant less to the men than it did to the women, and they had not expected the association to last indefinitely. Several of these unmarried mothers were socially insecure, lonely women who had knowingly invested themselves in an unpromising relationship, apparently hoping for little more than that it could be prolonged through their sexual involvement.[14]

It is frequently suggested that, because unmarried parents may use the sexual relationship to express unhealthy emotional needs, they are likely to encounter greater difficulty than others in their sexual experiences with each other. Actually, there is, understandably, very little information about the sexual needs of people who become unmarried parents. On the basis of the little that is known about their sexual behavior toward one another, their experiences seem to encompass a wide range. One young girl reports, "When it was over, we could hardly bear to look at each other. I wondered what all the shouting was about with sex. I think Dick felt the same way. Mostly we felt sorry for each other. It was awful." Yet for another, the sexual relationship was part of a sustained and deepening involvement that would probably have matched that of a good marriage.[15]

In or out of marriage, a sexual relationship can be used to meet healthy or unhealthy physical and emotional needs. A woman may use her sexual favors to gain whatever it is women sometimes hope to gain by offering or withholding their bodies. A man may make extravagant promises in order to obtain a woman's sexual favors. The sex act may be used essentially for sheer physical gratification, with little heed to the needs of the sex partner, or it can involve the highest degree of mutual fulfillment, representing a dedicated act of love. Judging by the attention sexual problems within marriage receive in our society, one must conclude that a substantial number of married couples probably suffer from sexual "hang-ups."

In the absence of supporting evidence, one cannot assume that people who become unmarried parents differ appreciably in their sexual needs from those who do not, or that their sexual experiences are less satisfying or less meaningful than other people's. One can expect perhaps that more unmarried couples are apt to have problems in sexual fulfillment because more of them are likely to be young and inexperienced, with their sexual encounters frequently taking place under adverse conditions. In other words, according to available evidence, men who are known to have become out-of-wedlock fathers do not appear to deviate noticeably in the way they select and relate to their sexual partners from those who are not known to have become out-of-wedlock fathers.

The Relationship Changes

With the conception of a child, a new dimension is introduced into the unmarried parents' relationship. People who were lovers now become prospective parents. It is no longer enough for them to think exclusively in terms of their feelings for each other. They must reassess their involvement in terms of their responsibility to the life that has been created out of their association. They must think about their families, about finances, about planning for the baby. They must consider what they now expect of themselves and of each other in a future relationship.

Unmarried men are likely to show a whole range of responses when they receive the knowledge that they are prospective fathers. They may become guilty, fearful, or hostile toward or solicitous of the unmarried mother. They may disavow all responsibility, they may show indifference, or they may offer to marry her. Of sixty-nine fathers in the Boston maternity home study who were informed of the pregnancy, two disappeared, five denied paternity, twenty ignored the unmarried mothers' efforts to reach them (although they were known to be in the area), four agreed reluctantly to contribute financially, twenty-four remained strongly supportive of the mother, and fourteen offered to marry her. In other words, approximately 60 per cent of those who knew they were prospective fathers saw themselves initially as emotionally or financially responsible.[16] Sauber and Rubinstein report that "over a third of the women had seen the putative father during pregnancy." [17]

Despite the initially favorable response on the part of many unmarried fathers, however, not many of the relationships survive the inevitable reassessment. One of the first casualties of the pregnancy is apt to be love, or what the unmarried parents had earlier perceived as love. In many instances, previous offers of marriage are quickly withdrawn by the man or are rejected by the woman.[18]

In re-evaluating each other as prospective parents or marriage partners, they may find they were not as much in love as they had thought; or they may realize that the relationship would not be able to withstand the stresses of parenthood, either in or out of wedlock. One partner may suddenly find the other wanting in important qualities. From the point at which they learn they have conceived a child, there is likely to be a gradual attrition in the relationship as time goes on until, following the birth of the baby, most will have lost contact with each other, except, of course, for the small percentage that eventuate in marriage.[19]

Although the break in the relationship is often by tacit or open agreement between the unmarried parents, there are points at which it is a decidedly one-sided affair. The unmarried father is likely to be the first to lose interest, and to lose it more decisively than the unmarried mother. As the pregnant woman becomes heavier, more ungainly, and more uncomfortable, and as she undergoes the loss in sex drive that often accompanies pregnancy, the unmarried father no longer sees her as the companion he knew. She becomes less attractive to him. As the first flush of guilt and fear subsides, so does the unmarried father's urge to help her. Visits and telephone calls become less frequent, and eventually comes the inevitable discontinuance of all contact.

In many instances the unmarried father's interest drops most noticeably at a time when the unmarried mother, responding with maternal interest to developments in the pregnancy, may long most for the attention of the man who fathered the child. It is at this point that she is likely to feel most acutely the maternal loneliness of her status as an unmarried parent. It is at this point that, despite her earlier inclinations to discontinue the relationship, the traditional concept of the absconding male and the deserted female is most poignant.[20]

The unmarried pregnant woman carries the physical, social, and emotional load, burdens that are spared the unmarried father. True, he may be unhappy about her circumstances and concerned about the baby, but he does not have to worry that "it" will show on him. He does not have to retire from society for the duration or invent stories about a spouse in military service. He does not have the physical discomforts of pregnancy. Unless the unmarried mother takes legal action against him, he can go about his normal activities uninterruptedly and is free to decide what his further involvement in unmarried parenthood is to be.

The unmarried mother, as the bearer of the visible evidence of their sexual relationship, has no choice but to remain involved. She needs the unmarried father much more than he needs her. For her self-esteem and emotional comfort, and for practical reasons, she needs to experience the continuing interest of the baby's father. It may be secondary to her at certain points whether his attention is prompted by love, by a sense of duty, by feelings of guilt, or by fear of legal action. The important thing for her is that he evidence interest in her and the baby.

In a way, the discontinuance of the relationship between the unmarried parents, although discomfiting to the woman, is in keeping with society's unspoken expectations. Society winks at the illicit sexual behavior, but looks with disfavor on the pregnancy that results from it. The censure that attaches to the pregnancy often rubs off on the relationship, exposing and emphasizing the unmarried parents' less attractive attributes in each other's eyes. In the absence of legal bonds to hold them together, the relationship becomes tainted, so to speak, and an association that might otherwise have continued for a while longer is abruptly terminated.

The Unmarried Father and the Agency

Agency perceptions of the role of the unmarried father and its relation to him range from total exclusion to near-total involvement. Some maternity homes, convinced that contact between a pregnant girl or woman and the father of her baby is inappropriate, do not permit visits between them. Others, including child welfare agencies, are convinced that the unmarried father can play an important role in their work with the unmarried mother and in the planning for the baby, and encourage him to participate actively. Traditionally, the unmarried father has not figured prominently as a parent to his out-of-wedlock child, or in the agency's planning for the child. His name rarely appears on the birth certificate. Agency planning for the child's future care has been almost exclusively with the mother.

On the assumption that every child has a right to know he was conceived of a father as well as of a mother, and to feel that his father was interested enough in his welfare to participate in planning for him, agencies have been making vigorous efforts to bring the unmarried father out of the shadows and to involve him more significantly in the planning for the child. The father is encouraged to come to the agency so that through direct observation and firsthand information it can get a more reliable picture of him than it thinks can be expected from the mother, and so that it can give the adoptive parents iinformation that, should he later inquire, can help the child establish a link with both his parental origins.[21] Some agencies request, in addition, an affidavit of paternity, or a written disavowal if the alleged father refuses to acknowledge paternity.

Some voluntary agencies have begun to take an active role in persuading the unmarried father to contribute to the unmarried mother's medical and living expenses and, where appropriate, to the costs of the child's care, particularly if there are reasons why the unmarried mother should not negotiate directly with him, or if she is timid about approaching him about money. This involvement is considered by some agencies to be both a practical necessity and a moral obligation. With the costs of health and welfare services continually rising, many unmarried mothers are unable to pay the full expenses of their care unaided. Since the unmarried mother fares badly at the hands of nature and society compared with the unmarried father, many people think that, in order to redress the balance, the unmarried father should pay in some way for his illicit sexual behavior. The most tangible way for him to pay is quite literally to pay in money. In addition to its practical value to the unmarried mother and the agency, and its moral value for the unmarried father, this tangible evidence of his sense of responsibility can sometimes bolster an unmarried mother's flagging self-esteem. Some agencies report that, in the course of his own involvement, the unmarried father can become more understanding of the difficulties involved for the woman having an out-of-wedlock child.

Whether an unmarried father is seen at the agency or not, the agency's interest in him can figure significantly in the mother's understanding of her situation. As she explores the worker's proposal that he be contacted and examines what she expects or hopes for from such a contact, or as she assesses her reasons for opposing it, she can also come to understand how her feelings about the baby's father may be affecting her attitude toward the baby, her dealings with her parents, and her perception of her own future. An agency's explanation of its requirement that the baby's father be involved in adoption planning can be an important factor in the mother's growing recognition of her baby's welfare as an individual apart from her own needs.

If the baby's father comes to the agency, and particularly if both parents are seen in joint session, an element of realism is injected into the unmarried mother's perception of her situation more rapidly than is likely to be the case without his involvement. Discussions about financial responsibility, about plans for the baby, and about their future relationship can bring into focus factors that previously may not have been clear to them.

An unmarried mother may recognize for the first time how precarious a future with the baby's father is likely to be as she hears him describe his unrealistic perceptions of himself as a husband and father, or as he expresses in the worker's presence the reluctance to marry that he has been unable to communicate directly to the unmarried mother. It will be recalled that it was only after Susan K. heard Ned express his doubts that she began to face the likelihood that he would not marry her. Not until Louanna witnessed Pete's unreasoning reaction in the interview with the worker could she take the full measure of his rejection of the baby and understand why he was willing to let her keep him.

On the other hand, a joint session can sometimes help the unmarried parents dispel the taint that has attached to their relationship because of the out-of-wedlock conception, and can help them to see that a sound marriage can still come of their union.

The Limits of Involvement

Not all unmarried fathers can or should be equally involved with agencies serving unmarried mothers and their children. In fact, some should not be involved at all. Much will depend upon the balance to be struck between the benefits expected from an individual father's participation and the other ramifications his participation can have. A major deterrent to involving an unmarried father is the harm it may do to others. Thus, most voluntary agencies, and some public agencies as well, try to protect a man's legitimate family either by not requiring a direct contact with him or by arranging it outside the agency, where detection is less likely.

An additional consideration is whether the benefits anticipated from an unmarried father's involvement are likely to be realized, particularly as compared with the effort required to obtain his co-operation. An example of this is the attempt by a public agency to get an unmarried father to contribute to his child's support or to the mother's expenses. It is generally thought that the unmarried mother, the child, the agency, and (if it is a tax-supported agency) the general public will benefit financially from such contributions. However, if it takes repeated efforts to get a man to maintain his payments, the cost may so far outstrip the amount he contributes that in the long run it is questionable whether anyone is the gainer.

Three reports point up some of the problems encountered in trying to collect support from unmarried fathers. One report, published in 1955, indicates:

Fathers subject to court orders for support contributed less frequently than fathers who had agreed to provide support. Only 47.1 per cent of the fathers subject to court orders contributed, compared with 66.2 per cent of fathers subject to agreements. . . . In the most informal type of arrangement, where the father and mother independently agreed on the amount of support, more than three-fourths of the fathers contributed . . .[22]

Ten years later Sauber and Rubinstein reported that "the overwhelming proportion of putative fathers who gave the unmarried mothers financial support did so voluntarily and without any legal action on the part of the mothers." [23]

Apparently the unmarried father's financial commitment is subject to considerable strain with the passing of time. "There is a clear correlation between the recency of the support order or agreement and the frequency of contributions. The contribution rate declined from 70.3 per cent for orders or agreements less than 6 months old to 38.3 per cent for orders or agreements made 3 years or more before the time of the study." [24]

According to Morlock a similar situation existed in 1928:

Records obtained by the Children's Bureau of collection of support orders show that the number of men who are in arrears in payments steadily increases with each year succeeding the date of the order. In one study made in 1928 the records showed that 44 per cent of the men whose orders to pay had been in force for from one to two years were in arrears, while no less than 73 per cent of those whose orders had been in force from five to seven years were in arrears.[25]

These findings do not necessarily prove that court orders are ineffectual or that the absence of a court order is the only factor in the more favorable outcomes of voluntary agreements. It may well be that an unmarried father's readiness to enter in a voluntary support agreement itself indicates a predisposition to contribute financially, particularly if he knows a voluntary agreement is likely to keep him out of court. No doubt, more money can be collected from some recalcitrant unmarried fathers with a court order than without one. These experiences do suggest, however, that, whatever the objective an agency may have in trying to involve an unmarried father, it is important to estimate the probable efficacy of the method it employs to achieve its goal.

Sometimes involving the unmarried father may be more of a liability than an asset to the unmarried mother. For example, unmarried mothers who rely on contributions from the baby's father for support may also need supplemental aid from public assistance. Many public assistance agencies deduct from the mother's total eligible grant the amount the father is to contribute. If he defaults and she applies for an increase (or for total support, if total support is what she needs), she may have to wait until her application has been processed and a decision made regarding further action against the father before she receives help. Pending a decision, she may have to get along on a reduced income, on small emergency grants, or sometimes on no income at all.

Some communities avoid such situations by having the father pay directly to the agency or court. Thus, the mother receives the full amount for which she is eligible, and the official agency takes responsibility for dealing with the father's delinquencies, eliminating any financial loss to the mother and child.

Requiring an unmarried mother to file a paternity complaint in order to establish eligibility for service from a public agency can create mental hardship for her. If the alleged father decides to contest the charge, he may marshal friendly witnesses to testify, rightly or wrongly, that they had sexual relations with her, thus impugning her allegations that he is the baby's father. Moreover, it is not unknown for the unmarried mother to be asked to describe, as part of her testimony to the court, the step-by-step events that presumably led to her becoming pregnant. At best, this is an unsavory procedure. At worst, it can be immeasurably harmful, not only to the unmarried mother but to the unmarried father and his witnesses, and to any others who, willy-nilly, may find themselves parties to such proceedings.

Sometimes an unmarried mother herself, with various motives, may ask that the unmarried father not be involved. She may want to spare him the discomfort of dealing with the agency; she may be concerned lest he give information she has withheld, or she may have other reasons for wanting to keep him out of the picture. Many agencies report that such objections are usually not difficult to overcome, and that if the worker is convinced it is important to involve the unmarried father, she will communicate her conviction to the unmarried mother, and in most instances the unmarried mother will give consent.[26] There is the danger, however, that the worker, in her desire to involve the unmarried father, may not be attuned to the unmarried mother's reactions. Mistaking compliance for acquiescence, the worker may underestimate the depth of the mother's feelings and fail to take into account the possible effect on her relationship with the agency.

Julia L.'s situation is a case in point. In itself, it does not contraindicate a policy of involving unmarried fathers with the agency, but suggests, rather, the dangers in a policy of strict enforcement. In a different context, it is reminiscent of the problem faced with Alice P. in connection with the request for care.[27] The question here is almost identical with the earlier one; namely, whether in a given situation the presumed future benefits to the child are likely to outweigh the more immediate potentially adverse effects on the mother.

Julia L., aged twenty-four, applied to a voluntary adoption agency when she was four months pregnant. Her manner was pleasant but detached, and there was an air of depression about her. She readily answered factual questions about the baby's father and for the most part painted a positive picture of his physical and mental traits. However, she did not respond to the worker's efforts to engage her in a discussion of her relationship with him prior to the pregnancy, or of his reactions to her being pregnant.

Julia asked a number of questions about adoption procedures, the selection of adoptive homes, the kinds of people who become adoptive parents, the age at which a child is placed, and so on. When the worker explained the agency's regulation about getting personal history directly from the father and asked permission to get in touch with him, Julia was frankly dismayed. With some agitation she explained that she had given a very full and accurate description of him. What other information would the agency like? She could not see why he had to be seen in person. She would rather they did not get in touch with him.

The reasons Julia was opposed to the agency's getting in touch with the baby's father could only be guessed at. It was not known what understanding she had had with him about the permanence of their relationship or what she was to expect of him if she should become pregnant. Nor was it known what support he had offered when he learned she was pregnant. One can surmise, however, that, whatever it was, it did not measure up to what she had expected it would or should be. Her encounters with him concerning these questions had apparently been bruising experiences for her, and she could not tolerate any discussion that touched on her relationship with him.

Julia was concerned about the baby. She wanted reassurance about the future to which she was consigning him by her contemplated relinquishment. She was obviously in deep distress.

The worker sympathized with Julia for not wanting the father involved, indicating that he had apparently disappointed her. However, it could mean a good deal to a child later on to have information about his heritage that had come directly from his birth father. The worker also pointed out that by seeing the father the agency could better match the baby with the adoptive family, that the agency did not feel justified in planning for a baby when it could not give what it considered optimum service.

Julia left with the understanding that she would think about signing the necessary consent. When she returned two weeks later, she agreed to sign the consent form and gave the necessary information for locating the father, remarking that she just hoped he would not get the idea that she had engineered this in order to re-establish contact with him.

Julia was seen irregularly after this—each time at the worker's initiative. She continued to be remote and mildly depressed, but consistently turned aside the worker's efforts to help her deal with her feelings about her experience with the baby's father. Three weeks after the birth of her daughter she signed surrender papers and asked to be notified when the baby was placed in an adoptive home. She did not ask whether the agency had been in touch with the father.

When Julia came to the agency, the last thing she wanted was further involvement of the baby's father in her affairs, particularly if it was to be at the behest of an agency after her own efforts had apparently failed. Her main concern was to make a suitable plan for the baby. If she could plan as a good mother for her child, it might in part offset the blow to her sense of herself as a woman that she had suffered because of the unhappy outcome of her association with the baby's father. Yet one of the first things she had to do if she was to provide responsibly for the baby was to consent to having the father brought into the situation. If she did not, her adequacy as a mother would, by implication, be impugned. Her resentment toward the baby's father became linked to the agency's requirement, and she was unable to involve herself in a treatment relationship that, in her mind, was closely associated with her feelings about him.

One cannot, of course, ascribe the whole of Julia's reactions to the issue of the involvement of the baby's father. Other factors may have contributed to her depression and withdrawal. She may have had a tendency toward depression, an underlying vulnerability that was reinforced by the pregnancy and her experience with the baby's father. It is conceivable that she would not have responded to offers of help even if she had not had to agree to the father's being seen. No doubt there are unmarried mothers who, once their initial objections have been overcome, can relate to the agency on a helping basis. It is important, however, to be alert in those situations in which involving the baby's father may do more harm than good.

A Person in His Own Right

Many practitioners, concerned about the unmarried father as a person with needs of his own, suggest that an agency's interest in him should extend beyond his responsibility to the unmarried mother and his illegitimate child, and that, wherever feasible, he should be offered help with other problems that may be troubling him.

Not all agencies offer the same degree of help. Some state frankly that, because of limited resources, they must give priority to the needs of unmarried mothers and their children. Even though they cannot offer extensive services to the unmarried father, they do strive to make his experience with the agency as constructive as possible for him.

Sometimes, in the course of defining his responsibilities, an unmarried father can be helped to clarify his feelings about the unmarried mother and the child. Occasionally, as a by-product, he may be better able to deal with other problems he is experiencing in connection with his out-of-wedlock parenthood—differences with his parents, if he is an adolescent; whether or how to inform his wife of his predicament, if he is a married man, and so on.

Some agencies suggest that, whether or not an unmarried father is helped with other problems, the mere fact that he has been given an opportunity to become involved with the agency can in itself be construed as a service to him, in that it enables him to exercise a few rights of his own, among them the right to be informed that he has begotten an illegitimate child, the right to know what plans are being made for the child, and the right to play a part in ensuring the child's future welfare. It is reported that many unmarried fathers, some of whom may at first have been reluctant to become involved, later express gratitude at having had the opportunity to do what they could for the unmarried mother as well as for the baby. Their participation helped to "resolve some of the guilt and confusion of unmarried parenthood." [28]

As agencies increasingly reach out to unmarried fathers, they are more and more likely to run into situations that do not fit established concepts of the unmarried father's role. An unmarried father may differ with the agency or with the unmarried mother as to what constitutes the best interests of his child. If agencies are to continue to invite the unmarried father's participation, they may have to revise their perceptions of what constitutes an appropriate role for him and of what their relationship with him should be.

For example, in the course of his negotiations with the agency an unmarried father may become interested in obtaining custody of his about-to-be-relinquished child. What is the obligation of an agency that has convinced the father of his importance as a birth-parent image and, in a sense, is responsible for having aroused his paternal feelings? Should he be perceived as a client, to be treated on a par with the mother? Is an agency likely to evaluate an unmarried father's wishes objectively if, up to this point, it has perceived him primarily in terms of the mother's relinquishment of the child? What happens to the agency's relationship with the unmarried mother if it does agree that the father's wish to have his child has merit? Of what practical use is it for the agency to concur with him if the law makes no provision for him to have custody of his child, other than through litigation?

A few agencies offer the unmarried father "help for his own sake," direct counseling services somewhat akin to those provided unmarried mothers. The hope is that, in addition to the personal help this affords him, it may also keep him from becoming involved in unwed parenthood again, either with the current partner or with another. It is sometimes suggested that agencies serving unmarried mothers should, when indicated, continue their contact with the unmarried father "after the pregnancy was terminated, the baby relinquished, and even . . . after the girl married and no longer remained in the picture," [29] as was reported in one case. This suggestion raises the question of how far help for the unmarried father should extend. Should it encompass the marital difficulties of the parents of an adolescent unmarried father? Should it include the wife who, tacitly encouraging her husband's philanderings, is in effect an accomplice in his unwed parenthood?

For all practical purposes, these questions may not be so urgent as are some others. Most of the agencies that have indicated they would like to serve unmarried fathers on a par with unmarried mothers admit they would not feel justified in doing so if it meant diverting limited staff from serving unmarried mothers. Moreover, they do not expect that the demands for such services, even if met, would be great enough to make serious inroads into services for unmarried mothers. Apparently most unmarried fathers are no more inclined to accept help with other than reality problems than are unmarried mothers.[30]

To be sure, it is important that agencies make it known—through active and relevant publicity, individual contacts, and other means—that they are interested in more than just getting unmarried fathers to shoulder their responsibilities. The trouble is that people seem increasingly to be equating "aggressive reaching out" with the use of authority. Frequently offers of help become interlaced with hints at legal action if the unmarried father should fail to respond to the agency's overtures. The result often is that what was supposed to have been a reaching out with an offer of help may turn into a threat to prosecute if the unmarried father should remain unco-operative. For example: "We also suggested that the father's involvement might help avoid undesired legal action and might facilitate the handling of the situation under more favorable circumstances," [31] and "Legal implications, such as statutory rape, etc., may have to be explained at the worker's discretion, to impress upon the unmarried father the importance of making an appointment with the agency." [32]

If an agency is legally authorized to act on behalf of an unmarried mother, and if it intends to use this authority against an unco-operative unmarried father—or if it encourages an unmarried mother to take legal action—its image as a helping agent is likely to lose much of its meaning to the unmarried father. Under the circumstances he may find it difficult to reconcile the agency's offer of help with its threat of legal action and may, in fact, wonder whether the agency's intent is to work with him or against him.

Part of the confusion may be due to a failure to identify the purpose of the use of authority. Is it in order to give an unmarried father help for his own sake? Is it meant to make him face up to the consequences of his sexual behavior by requiring him to contribute financially (or in emotional support) to promote the agency's work with the unmarried mother?

Admittedly, these questions are interdependent and often overlap. Action in response to one may have its reverberations on another. For example, it may be that requiring a man to make restitution for his sexual peccadilloes will improve his character and make him feel better. These questions cannot always be considered in relation to each other, however, as there are times when they need to be dealt with separately. If collecting money from an unmarried father can sometimes improve his character, there are also occasions when money should be collected from him whether it improves his character or not.

A question for the agency is whether it can function simultaneously as helper and as disciplinarian to the same person. Undoubtedly this sometimes can be done. The constructive use of authority and aggressive reaching out has been demonstrated in other connections. However, each of the functions is likely to be more effective if the agency's intent is clear. Failure to distinguish, when necessary, between an unmarried father's need for help with other problems and his obligation to the unmarried mother and their child may detract from the agency's effectiveness in either or both roles. A further question is whether an authoritative position can appropriately be taken by a social agency that is not ordinarily perceived by the public as having such a role, especially if an unmarried father is not under court order. This question would apply particularly to a voluntary agency.

In some ways the ambiguities in the relationships of social agencies with unmarried fathers reflect some of the contradictions in society's attitudes.

Society's Paradox

Among the many contradictions with which society approaches the unmarried father are those pertaining to his rights as a father. In many states an adjudication of paternity, although obligating him for child support (sometimes for the support of the unmarried mother also), may deny him the right to decision regarding plans for the child, visitation, and custody, except as the mother permits. "Although it is a cardinal principle that the welfare of the child should determine its custody, it is usually held that the mother of an illegitimate child has a legal right to custody superior to that of the father." [33] This point of view can mean that the mother not only has prior claim to keep the child with her, but also that she can turn him over, often without the father's knowledge, to others—to a social agency for adoption, to relatives, or to friends—without having to prove a priori that such a plan is in the best interests of the child or that it is better than giving the father custody.[34]

Ironically, sometimes the right to the child that is denied an unmarried father by law can be granted to him by the mother. She can "give" him the child without official inquiry into his suitability as a parent or into the conditions under which the child is likely to live. Without legal sanction for the father's custody, the mother can take the child back at any time. If the child is a focus of conflict between the parents, there is the danger, as sometimes happens in divorce, that he may become "an item thrown into the parents' negotiations, . . . bartered for various concessions having nothing to do with his personal welfare." [35] Thus, the withholding of custody from the father "in the best interests of the child" may turn out to be in the child's worst interests. It may deny him the protection of a stable home that might be his if the father were granted legal custody in the first place.

It is difficult to estimate how frequently informal unprotected arrangements are made between unmarried parents. Nor is it known what proportion of unmarried fathers would request custody of a child whom the mother intends to relinquish. Opinions about unmarried fathers' interest in their out-of-wedlock children range from "only rarely does an unmarried father wish to keep his out-of-wedlock child" [36] to "some fathers come close to nervous collapse when their girl friends give their babies up for adoption." [37] One agency reports that 4 per cent of unmarried fathers who were referred to a special project kept their out-of-wedlock children.[38] Perhaps the exact numbers are not so important as are the consequences for the individual unmarried father and illegitimate child who, because of legal anomalies, are denied the benefits of a parent-child relationship.

Time for a Change

The picture is changing, however. The rights of out-of-wed-lock fathers are being tested and determined in the several states. Increasingly, courts are awarding custody of illegitimate children to fathers who petition for it, on the assumption that there may be situations in which the best interests of the illegitimate child may dictate that the father rather than the mother should have custody.[39]

For the most part these changes are taking place through court action, and since court action is likely to entail lengthy and costly litigation, the chances of a man's obtaining custody of his child are considerably reduced if he cannot afford the costs of litigation. Thus, although technically the law applies equally to all, the rights of the father and the best interests of the child may be determined by the father's economic circumstances rather than by the validity of his claim and the welfare of the child.

A few states have begun to consider regularizing some aspects of the unmarried father's rights through legislation. So far such attempts have not met with much success. A bill introduced into the New York State Legislature that would have given some unmarried fathers prior custody rights under limited conditions died in committee. It was observed, however, that "the very fact that it was brought up at all is a sign of hope for the future." [40]

In some respects the unmarried father's responsibilities are as ambiguous as his rights. Except in special cases, such as rape or when minors are involved, there are no legal provisions by which all unmarried fathers are required to acknowledge paternity of illegitimate children. Some do so voluntarily under the aegis and protection of a social agency. Others establish paternity by adjudication through court action or through the intervention of a tax-supported agency that is serving the unmarried mother or the child. Inevitably a substantial number of unmarried fathers do not establish paternity—*i.e.,* those who abscond, those who do not comply with the voluntary agency's request for an affidavit of paternity, those associated with unmarried mothers not receiving agency care, and those who are not required to acknowledge paternity "for casework or other reasons."

Thus, a substantial number of illegitimate children are deprived of a right that is increasingly looked on as essential to their future well-being, the "right to the interest of his father, and, if the child should desire it, knowledge about him at a suitable age." [41] Yet if knowledge about his father is as essential to a child's welfare as it is said to be, it should not be left to the accident of a parent's association with an agency or to the whim of his father. It should be a matter of public concern, with the rights of every illegitimate child equally protected by law, barring those situations in which the welfare of the unmarried parents, the child, or innocent bystanders would be in jeopardy.

Society's ambivalence toward the unmarried father is further illustrated in the conduct of paternity proceedings. In most states a man is allegedly an *alleged* father until he has been adjudged actual father of the child—that is, "innocent until proved guilty." Paternity proceedings are presumably civil actions. Yet the quasi-criminal character of the hearings is unmistakable.[42] One has the impression that an alleged father may sometimes have been adjudicated practically on being named, particularly if he is associated with an unmarried mother who must have help from a public agency.

In a way, social agencies may be helping to perpetuate some of the inconsistencies and inequities in the laws pertaining to unmarried fathers. By offering a man the opportunity to settle his paternity problems outside the legal machinery, an agency is saying in effect that it considers the machinery inappropriate to the task, possibly even harmful. In other words, the official system is something to be avoided, if possible. Clearly, then, the system needs to be improved. Yet so long as a few privileged unmarried fathers can have immunity through the protection of an agency, the impetus toward change is not likely to be vigorous.

Those who cannot avoid tangling with the legal system do not enjoy such protection. Frequently they are the unmarried fathers, mentioned above, who are apt to become involved in paternity adjudications, on the basis of which they may be assessed for child support for the duration of the child's minority. If the father is of a racial or ethnic minority, his earning capacity may be conditioned by limited education, inadequate occupational skills, low salary, irregular employment, racial discrimination, and the like. Paradoxically, the system comes down hardest on those who can least afford it. It tries "to obtain payments from men without money, in a social context that encourages the unmarried mother to conceal the identity of the putative father." [43]

The more one considers the problems of out-of-wedlock paternity, the clearer it becomes that laws and procedures by which paternity is established, child support assessed, and custody and other parental rights determined need to be changed. It should be possible for unmarried parents (and their parents, when indicated) to negotiate in privacy and with dignity, and with regard for the protection of all those involved in the proceedings. Paternity hearings need to be divested of their quasi-criminal attributes. "Legislation should provide for action to establish paternity as a civil rather than a criminal procedure, and should permit a father to appear before a court without trial to acknowledge paternity and to agree to provide for the support of his child." [44]

Child support should be assessed according to the unmarried father's ability to pay, and toughness or compassion should be meted out according to the needs of the child and of the unmarried mother, and with due respect for the father's rights as well as his responsibilities, regardless of social class, color, economic status, or other nonrelevant considerations. In other words, society needs to narrow the gap between the unmarried fathers it protects and those it punishes.

As the definition of legitimacy is broadened and as legitimation is made easier,[45] the status of the child born out of wedlock is more and more likely to parallel that of the child involved in a divorce. In some respects the protections provided the latter can apply to the illegitimate child, who can be considered part of a "putative family" during the negotiations.[46]

One can probably expect, or at least hope, that increasingly the principles that govern custody, visitation, and the like, for the child of divorce will be extended to the child born out of wedlock. In reference to the use of impartial custody investigations by courts to protect the interests of the child in divorce proceedings, it is suggested that "custody and support awards . . . be based on the best interests of the child rather than simply on a mechanical rule for allocation according to the sex or position of the spouses [parents] or on a rubber-stamp agreement made by the parents." [47]

Changes in the law are likely to bring corresponding changes in social agency practice. If agencies are relieved of having to compensate, through services to individual unmarried fathers, for conditions that should be corrected through legislative action, they are likely to be in a position to define their roles toward unmarried fathers more clearly. With the protection of the unmarried mother and the out-of-wedlock child provided for by law, and with the unmarried father's rights and responsibilities legally defined, some social agencies might well perceive themselves as giving services to both unmarried parents in the broad sense.

The unmarried father could then become party to negotiations on a par with the unmarried mother. With the welfare of the child the focus of concern, there would be no fixed commitment to any one plan, or to either parent for custody of the child or the right to plan for him. It is not inconceivable that, as a resource for unmarried mothers and fathers, an agency could serve an unmarried father whether he was associated with an unmarried mother in its care or not. He could then be helped with psychological problems and with practical problems, such as finding work or continuing his education. The agency could function as a kind of multiservice center for unmarried parents.

It is difficult to tell how long it may be before significant legislative changes can be expected. As long as influential segments of society remain hostile or ambivalent toward those who have children out of wedlock, progress will probably be limited to the small expensive gains achieved through individual litigation or through the faint hope that resides in a bill that has "died in legislative committee." Unmarried fathers do not have legislative representation as a pressure group and must depend upon social workers, attorneys, and other concerned citizens to act on their behalf and "push the law to correct the inequities that now exist." [48] Some beginning steps, already taken, point the way.

The National Conference of Lawyers and Social Workers is bringing the two professions together on a national level. Why cannot such conferences be set up on a local level? Getting social workers, lawyers, and legislators together to examine the social and legal aspects of illegitimacy is at least one step—and a very important one—in trying to find solutions of the many problems involved.[49]

It is not an easy task. When one is familiar with the many ramifications of illegitimacy, as are social workers, lawyers, and others, ambivalence toward unmarried parents, particularly toward unmarried fathers, can sometimes be acute. Yet unless we can acknowledge these ambivalences and learn to deal with them in our professions, we, too, are likely to drag our feet.

NOTES

1. Percy Gamble Kammerer, *The Unmarried Mother: A Study of Five Hundred Cases* (Boston: Little, Brown, and Company, 1918), p. 302.
2. Maud Morlock, "Establishment of Paternity," *Proceedings of the National Conference of Social Work, 1940* (New York: Columbia University Press, 1940), pp. 363–76.
3. Some notable early exceptions were Vista Del Mar Child-Care Service, Los Angeles, and St. Elizabeth's Infant Hospital, San Francisco. See Reuben Pannor, Fred Massarik, and Byron W. Evans, *The Unmarried Father: Demonstration and Evaluation of an Assertive Casework Approach* (Los Angeles: Vista Del Mar Child-Care Service, 1967); and Sister Ann, D.C., "Counseling the Unmarried Father," paper presented at National Conference on Social Welfare, San Francisco, May 1959.

4. The studies are based on experiences with different segments of the unmarried father population or with their unmarried mother partners. The unmarried fathers included in the studies are those known through maternity homes, most of whose clients, largely white and middle class, release their babies for adoption; those known to voluntary adoption agencies; those known to a public adoption agency with mixed clientele; and those associated with a group of unmarried mothers who kept their babies, the vast majority of whom were Negro or Puerto Rican. There was also information about unmarried fathers who had been associated with unmarried mothers interviewed in a follow-up study. Some were white, some Negro. Some had kept their babies; others had relinquished theirs.

As can be expected with a subject that presents as formidable research problems as does unmarried parenthood, the studies have various limitations. Moreover, they differ in the size and the representativeness of the sample, in the scope of the investigation, and, in some instances, in the rigor of the research approach. However, there are points of agreement among them. Unless this agreement is essentially a compounding of the same error from one study to the next, the findings can be useful both in planning further studies and in indicating probable areas of common experience among many different kinds of unmarried fathers.

5. Elizabeth Herzog, "Some Notes About Unmarried Fathers," *Child Welfare* 45 (April 1966), p. 195.

6. "Research on Unmarried Fathers: Are They Different in Personality?" *NCI* (National Council on Illegitimacy) *Newsletter* 8 (Fall 1968), 4; from a paper entitled "Fathers of Children Conceived Out-of-Wedlock: An Analysis of Pre-Pregnancy, High School, Psychological Test Results," by Jerome D. Pauker (presented at the Annual Meeting of the Midwestern Psychological Association, Chicago, 1968).

7. Mignon Sauber and Elaine Rubinstein, *Experiences of the Unwed Mother as a Parent: A Longitudinal Study of Unmarried Mothers Who Keep Their First-Born* (New York: Community Council of Greater New York, 1965), p. 26.

8. Charles E. Bowerman, Donald F. Irish, and Hallowell Pope, *Unwed Motherhood: Personal and Social Consequences* (Chapel Hill: University of North Carolina, 1963), p. 94.

9. Rose Bernstein, "One Hundred Unmarried Mothers and Their Problems," unpublished study (Boston: Crittenton Hastings House, 1961–63), p. 68a.

10. Bowerman, Irish, and Pope, *Unmarried Parenthood*, pp. 96–99; Sauber and Rubinstein, *Experiences of the Unwed Mother*, p. 27.

11. Bowerman, Irish, and Pope, *Unmarried Parenthood*, pp. 108, 109, 120; Pannor, Massarik, and Evans, *The Unmarried Father*, pp. 34, 39; Sauber and Rubinstein, *Experiences of the Unwed Mother*, p. 25; Clark E. Vincent, *Unmarried Mothers* (New York: Free Press of Glencoe, 1961), pp. 74–76.

12. Kammerer, *The Unmarried Mother*, p. 304.

13. Three Studies (Bernstein, "One Hundred Unmarried Mothers"; Bowerman, Irish, and Pope, *Unmarried Parenthood;* and Pannor, Massarik, and Evans, *The Unmarried Father*) report similar findings on the prepregnancy relationship. Pannor report that the unmarried fathers' assessment of the relationship was similar to that of the unmarried mothers'.

14. Bernstein, "One Hundred Unmarried Mothers," p. 60.

15. *Ibid.* See also Vincent, *Unmarried Mothers,* pp. 32–35.

16. Bernstein, "One Hundred Unmarried Mothers," p. 62.

17. Sauber and Rubinstein, *Experiences of the Unwed Mother,* p. 35.

18. Bernstein, "One Hundred Unmarried Mothers"; and Bowerman, Irish, and Pope, *Unmarried Parenthood*, pp. 151, 152.

19. It may be that this description, based primarily on the Bernstein and Pannor studies, applies mainly to unmarried parents whose babies are released for adoption. The Sauber and Rubinstein findings, based on an unmarried mother population that was 87 per cent Negro and Puerto Rican, the vast majority of whom kept their babies, reports considerably less attrition in the relationship between the unmarried parents, particularly as expressed in the unmarried father's continued voluntary financial support. It may be that class and color influence the relationship during pregnancy and after, much as they do the plan for the baby. See Sauber and Rubinstein, *Experiences of the Unwed Mother,* pp. 51–56.

20. Bernstein, "One Hundred Unmarried Mothers," p. 63.

21. This point of view is presented in: Elizabeth Anglim, "The Adopted Child's Heritage—Two Natural Parents," *Child Wel-*

fare 44 (June 1965), pp. 339–43; Linda C. Burgess, "The Unmarried Father in Adoption Planning," *Children* 15 (March-April 1968), pp. 71–74; Catherine Boling, "The Putative Father," *Child Welfare* 43 (July 1964), pp. 368–71; and Hal K. Platts, "A Public Adoption Agency's Approach to Natural Fathers," *Child Welfare* 47 (November 1968), pp. 530–37.

22. U.S. Department of Health, Education, and Welfare, *Support from Absent Fathers of Children Receiving ADC,* Public Assistance Report no. 41, prepared for the Social Security Administration by Saul Kaplan (Washington, D.C.: Government Printing Office, 1955), p. 35.

23. Sauber and Rubinstein, *Experiences of the Unwed Mother,* p. 89.

24. Kaplan, *Support from Absent Fathers,* p. 36.

25. Morlock, "Establishment of Paternity," p. 368.

26. Burgess, "The Unmarried Father," p. 72; Pannor, Massarik, and Evans, *The Unmarried Father,* p. 62; and Platts, "A Public Adoption Agency's Approach," p. 533.

27. See Chapter 2.

28. Anglim, "The Adopted Child's Heritage," p. 342.

29. Sister Ann, D.C., "Counseling the Unmarried Father."

30. Pannor, Massarik, and Evans, *The Unmarried Father,* pp. 97–98.

31. Platts, "A Public Adoption Agency's Approach," p. 533.

32. Pannor, Massarik, and Evans, *The Unmarried Father,* p. 51.

33. Freda Jane Lippert, "The Need for a Clarification of the Putative Father's Legal Rights," *Journal of Family Law* 8 (Fall 1968), p. 403.

34. Sanford N. Katz, "Legal Protections for the Unmarried Mother and Her Child," *Children* 10 (March-April 1963), p. 58.

35. Walter Wadlington, "The Courts and Children's Rights," *Children* 16 (July-August 1969), p. 140.

36. Burgess, "The Unmarried Father," p. 73.

37. Judy Klemesrud, "The Unwed Father, Long Ignored, Now Gets Counseling, Too," New York *Times,* July 25, 1969, p. 56.

38. Platts, "A Public Adoption Agency's Approach," p. 535.

39. For a review of court decisions pertaining to custody and other rights of unmarried fathers, See Lippert, "The Need for a Clarification," pp. 403–411.

40. Karl D. Zukerman, "Social Attitudes and the Law," in *The*

Double Jeopardy, The Triple Crisis—Illegitimacy Today (New York: National Council on Illegitimacy, 1969), pp. 75–76.

41. *Child Welfare League of America Standards for Services to Unmarried Parents* (New York: Child Welfare League of America, 1960), p. 27.

42. Katz, "Legal Protections," p. 56.

43. Elizabeth Herzog, "Some Notes About Unmarried Fathers," p. 197.

44. *CWLA Standards*, p. 64.

45. See Lippert, "The Need for a Clarification," pp. 411–413.

46. *Ibid.*, p. 415.

47. Wadlington, "The Courts and Children's Rights," pp. 140–141.

48. Zukerman, "Social Attitudes and the Law," p. 77.

49. *Ibid.*, pp. 77–78.

7

SOME
PERSISTENT
ISSUES

Communities have been perennially troubled by the problem of how to make optimum use of resources which, in most instances, are insufficient to meet the demand for them. The question has become more urgent recently because many agencies report that they may have to curtail their services to unmarried mothers because of lack of funds. An agency or community that is contemplating major changes in its services is often in a good position to take stock of past performances, to re-examine its definition of need, to identify superfluous activities, to reinterpret agency functions, and to redirect its resources so that unmarried mothers can have access to the services they need.

Improving and Extending Services

One of the primary requirements in maximizing services to unmarried mothers is to broaden the perception of need and to distinguish between those needs that derive specifically from a woman's having an out-of-wedlock child and those that she has in common with people whose unmet needs are related to other circumstances: they are poor and pregnant, they are working mothers or heads of one-parent families, they are adolescents, and so forth. Sometimes the need for special services for the unmarried mother may be as much an indictment of existing services for people with other problems as it is an indication of the unmarried mother's special needs. Thus, a settlement house that institutes a recreation program for adolescent unmarried mothers is soon flooded with requests for admission from young married mothers who are also bored, lonely, and burdened prematurely with the responsibilities of child care. The staff of a comprehensive care program finds itself in the embarrassing position of having to turn away a nonpregnant schoolgirl who has heard that their school is much better than hers. Efforts to improve prenatal care for unmarried mothers often reveals many married women who also receive inadequate prenatal care. Thus, it is noted:

. . . while some 5,000 babies were born out-of-wedlock to women without benefit of proper medical care, about 27,000 were born to married women who also did not have adequate care. . . . We should note that if young mothers are at risk, many more of them are married than are unmarried. In other words, if we fix attention too closely on special groups, we will be in danger of losing larger targets.

It might be useful to ask at this point, if our approach to the problem of adequate provision and use of maternal and child services has not been moved off center by the magnetic attraction of illegitimacy.[1]

It should not be necessary for a girl or woman to become illegitimately pregnant in order to obtain decent schooling, better nutrition, adequate prenatal care, interesting recreation, and other services that may have been out of her reach previously. And what about the unmet needs of males, who cannot be rescued via an out-of-wedlock pregnancy?

Another matter that needs to be re-examined is the way psychological counseling services for unmarried mothers are used. On the theory that nonmarital pregnancy is related to unresolved emotional conflict, it is also assumed by some practitioners that unmarried mothers should have help for the problems that may have led to the pregnancy. It is hoped that, through an understanding of these emotional conflicts, the psychological and social hazards for the unmarried mother can be reduced and her having another out-of-wedlock pregnancy prevented.

As has been mentioned earlier, most unmarried mothers do not take kindly to excursions into their psychological past or into the reasons for their having become pregnant. Probing efforts by the helping person often result in a silent tug-of-war as the unmarried mother tries to avoid a service that she does not want and that is supposed to correct a problem she does not think she has (or does not wish to acknowledge) except insofar as the helping person insists. In many instances the professional energy expended in trying to persuade the unmarried mother to accept the proffered service yields only equivocal results.

Most unmarried mothers are in contact with the social agency for approximately six weeks (sometimes less) to six months prior to delivery. Most of them terminate contact following the conclusion of a plan for the baby. Six months or less is a relatively short time in which to try to uncover and deal with underlying psychological problems that are thought to be related to an out-of-wedlock pregnancy. If, by the time the unmarried mother has left agency care, substantial progress has not been made toward resolving some of the problems that have been probed, she may be left with many emotional raw spots and few usable insights, and may be no better off psychologically than she was before treatment was attempted. Moreover, undue emphasis on the pathological implications of a nonmarital pregnancy can generate a climate of emotional illness that may reinforce an unmarried mother's already demeaned sense of herself.

The preoccupation with psychological causation has communicated itself, via the popular literature and the mass media, to many of the unmarried mothers themselves. Frequently this emphasis serves only to divert their psychic energies from current problems that have to be dealt with and encourages an unhealthy avoidance of realities. Sometimes the girl who comes to an agency seemingly well motivated to learn about the psychological reasons for her out-of-wedlock pregnancy may only be echoing what she has heard and read. Schooled in the language of psychodynamics, she offers explanations that she thinks the helping person would like to hear.

As Seeley observes, "The explicit awareness of high-school kids . . . of the depth-psychological world they now inhabit is exquisite, and many of them know their gamesmanship better than the adults." [2] Often treatment of the knowledgeable unmarried mother ends where it began—with the claim that she became pregnant because of a poor relationship with her parents.

No doubt some out-of-wedlock pregnancies do represent efforts by the unmarried mother to cope with emotional conflicts she has been unable to resolve through other means. However, an analysis of available evidence by an eminent researcher challenges this point of view as a general hypothesis regarding the causes of illegitimacy:

The results of these studies do not support the sweeping generalizations about out-of-wedlock pregnancy often reported in the literature. . . . Problems of design and method that stand in the way of some of these conclusions include lack of adequate control groups, use of questionable evaluation methods, and use of samples so select that little generalizing can be done. One major source of error . . . is that the information upon which conclusions are based comes so often from the statements and other behavior of unmarried mothers already experiencing reactions to their unmarried pregnant state. [3]

Traditionally the services just described have been available primarily to residents of maternity homes and, more recently, to participants in a few comprehensive care programs. The total thus served is not likely to exceed 15 or 20 per cent of all unmarried mothers. Frequently the same population is offered several varieties of psychological help simultaneously: casework, psychiatric treatment, group work, group therapy, and the like. In most instances these services engage the efforts of a community's costly and highly skilled practitioners—trained social workers, psychologists, and psychiatrists—who are usually also in short supply. One must question whether this concentration of scarce, specialized services on such a small percentage of unmarried mothers constitutes the most appropriate use of a community's resources when vast numbers of unmarried mothers receive minimal services or none at all.

One of the more persistent concerns over the years has been the maldistribution of social services to unmarried mothers, the vast majority of whom do not receive essential services: shelter, help in planning for the baby, legal help, psychological counseling, and the like. The last available national survey indicates that public and voluntary child welfare agencies serve approximately one out of every six women who have out-of-wedlock babies in a year. Maternity homes serve one in ten. If allowance is made for those who are served by family agencies, hospital social service departments, comprehensive care programs for adolescents, and a few AFDC programs, the proportion served may be one-third at most, leaving approximately two-thirds of all unmarried mothers without basic social services. Furthermore, social agencies serve one in three white unmarried mothers and one in ten black unmarried mothers. Maternity homes serve one in ten white unmarried mothers and one in fifty black unmarried mothers.[4] (Unserved or minimally served unmarried mothers may also be Indian, Mexican-American, or Puerto Rican, depending upon the region of the country.)

The figures do not seem to have changed appreciably since the survey on which they are based was conducted, except that there may have been a slight rise in services to black unmarried mothers in the last few years. Conditions vary from state to state. In some states racial inequities in services to unmarried mothers are relatively mild; in others the problem is acute.

One of the influences underlying the distribution of services to unmarried mothers has been the assumption that the social consequences of illegitimacy differ according to race; that having an out-of-wedlock child entails psychological and social hazards for the white unmarried mother, whereas there is little or no shame or social penalty for the black unmarried mother. Often these assumptions have been used to justify or reinforce policies based on racial prejudice and discrimination. Thus, it is taken for granted that the white unmarried mother should have resources for hiding her pregnancy and disposing of the baby; namely, maternity home care and adoption services, resources that are considered unnecessary for the black unmarried mother. In many communities little effort is made to inform Negro unmarried mothers of these services. In some communities they are discouraged from using these services.

The fact that the adoption market for black babies has been small compared to the adoption market for white babies, and that few Negro unmarried mothers have been able to pay for maternity home care, has nourished the conviction that keeping the baby, besides being a practical necessity, is actually the plan of choice for most Negro unmarried mothers. These assumptions must be explored and assessed in the light of recent developments if services for unmarried mothers are to be more equitably distributed than they currently are in many communities.

Some practitioners are under the impression that there has been a trend recently toward a leveling of attitudes of blacks and whites toward illegitimacy; that a larger percentage of Negro unmarried mothers are asking to relinquish their babies for adoption, whereas more white unmarried mothers are keeping theirs. By the same token, it seems that fewer white unmarried mothers and more black unmarried mothers are thought to be concerned about concealment. Some ten years ago it was noted that less than three-quarters of the white girls admitted to a maternity home during a six-month period asked for shelter for purposes of concealment. Some of the other reasons for requesting admission were to keep an adolescent separated from the baby's father, to keep knowledge of the girl's pregnancy from an ailing grandparent, to provide housing and companionship for a lonely out-of-state woman, to provide supervision and schooling for a teen-ager, to reduce family tensions generated by the pregnant girl's presence, and to provide health supervision for the protection of mother and baby.

Often the staff is more vigorous about concealing the residents' identities than are the residents themselves.[5]

Applications to a maternity home for Negro unmarried mothers are reported to have exceeded the bed accommodations by four to one. Forty per cent of the residents requested adoption outright, and it was estimated that 60 per cent or more would have requested such service if they had thought adoptive homes would be available. The first responses to a publicity campaign for the recruitment of adoptive homes for Negro babies in a large city came from black unmarried mothers who wished to relinquish their babies.[6] In other words, when Negro unmarried mothers are informed about maternity homes and when they think there is some chance that their babies will be adopted, many more are likely to apply for these services.

A comparison of adoption and birth control in a family planning program in Alabama produced the observation that "it is one of the fundamental principles of adoption that adoption takes place only *after* individuals are informed and have weighed the advantages and the disadvantages of this new idea in light of the information."[7]

This discussion is not meant to suggest that there is any particular virtue in a black unmarried mother's emulating whites in her reaction to having an out-of-wedlock child. It is rather to point out that when some of our assumptions about attitudes toward illegitimacy in relation to color are examined critically, they break down at so many points that they become untenable as a basis for allocating services.

Admittedly the problem of adoption services to Negro unmarried mothers is not the responsibility of the social welfare community alone. The whole of our economic and social structure is involved. Black babies cannot be placed in adoption because the black middle class, from which adoptive homes have traditionally been recruited, is not large enough to provide a sufficient number of homes for those babies who need them. As it is, Negro families have overadopted in relation to their income. It is to be expected that, if the economic circumstances of Negroes improves, the number of black adoptive homes will increase. One of the large outlets for black babies exists in an area of a Southern state that contains a sizable black middle-class population. It is recognized, of course, that the use of nonblack adoptive homes can partially solve the problem. Realistically, however, matching for color is likely to continue as an important factor in the adoption placement of babies for many years to come.

Many agencies and communities have been establishing programs for correcting the imbalance in the distribution of services for unmarried mothers. A few of the programs have been mentioned earlier in connection with adolescent unmarried mothers and aftermath problems. Other programs provide for interracial and subsidized adoptions, interagency adoption exchanges, and permanent foster family homes for the placement of previously "hard-to-place" children; [8] group approaches; [9] the differential use of manpower; [10] increased services to unmarried mothers who keep their babies; special projects in public child welfare agencies; the extension of maternity home services through the use of foster family homes, wage homes, and outclient care; the establishment of halfway houses; and community-wide efforts for more effective co-ordination of services.

Changes in the function of maternity homes, if put into effect, may also open new vistas in services to unmarried mothers. With increasing emphasis on social, psychological, and health rehabilitation, and decreasing focus on shelter for concealment, maternity homes would be in a position to meet a variety of needs for unmarried mothers.[11] Residence could be available to those who need corrective health experiences to offset the ill-effects of a lifetime of poor nutrition, to those who could benefit from a respite from overcrowded and tension-packed homes, to those whose special educational needs cannot be met in the community, and to those who need psychological counseling. It is hoped that there will always be room for unmarried mothers whose primary need is, or is thought to be, protection through concealment.

As centers for rehabilitation, maternity homes are likely to attract many more than the 10 per cent of unmarried mothers currently served in the 200 or so existing shelters, all of which are voluntarily supported. It is doubtful that such an expanded demand could be met under voluntary auspices. Nor should this be expected. Unmarried motherhood entails health and welfare hazards for mother and baby. As such, it has many of the features of a public health problem and must be regarded as a public responsibility. If the need for maternity home services is to be met adequately, it will have to be through tax-supported facilities. Yet in not one of the fifty states in the United States is there a single publicly sponsored maternity home. It is hard to believe that this most urgently needed service for a population of mothers and children at risk remains in the province of a private enterprise.

One way of promoting maximum use of a community's existing resources is through the elimination of some of the unnecessary motions involved in duplicated efforts. Recognizing that it is wasteful for an unmarried mother who has applied to the wrong agency or who needs more than one type of service simultaneously to have to repeat her request or establish eligibility for each service separately, some communities have, from time to time, experimented with some form of centralized referral service. A community agency, either an already existing one or one created for the purpose, is designated the core agency through which all requests for service for unmarried mothers are routed. On the basis of information from the applicant or referring person, the core agency directs the unmarried mother to the agency it considers most appropriate to her need. Negotiations are usually handled by telephone, although they may occasionally involve a personal interview. Despite the benefits expected from such an arrangement, a number of projects, although reported to have achieved their purposes, were nevertheless discontinued after a number of years, seemingly without explanation.

It is sometimes difficult to determine and assess from a written report the reasons for the demise of a program. Often the salient factors are not spelled out and have to be inferred by the reader. A between-the-lines reading of reports from several centralized referral projects indicates that total co-ordination of all relevant health and welfare services is crucial and that total co-ordination can be achieved only if key agencies are prepared to relinquish some of their individual autonomy to the total program. This means that each agency must be willing to accept the judgment of the core agency. The refusal of one or two key agencies to accept referrals deemed appropriate by the central agency can spell failure for an otherwise carefully worked out project. If problems of co-ordination involve interagency and interprofessional rivalries, as they sometimes do, it would be well for the agencies to take time to iron out relationship problems before initiating the actual service. Prior preparation of this kind often pays for itself later in a more effective service and a more lasting program.

In one of the more enduring programs, established some fifteen years ago in Connecticut, a considerable period was devoted to this phase before unmarried mothers were accepted for service. On the basis of continuing discussions, practitioners from many different services were able to learn about each other: social workers, doctors, hospital nurses, public health nurses, lawyers, clergymen, school officials and teachers, and police-women. They were amazed at what they did not know about each other's work, and at how little they had realized what each could contribute toward improving services for unmarried mothers. With this new understanding, they were able to establish a co-ordinated service whereby an unmarried mother could receive help through a single application. On the basis of information she gave to one agency, and with the unmarried mother's consent, the physician or social worker, depending upon which service she applied for first, could make a referral on her behalf to the other service.[12]

Unless all relevant agencies are prepared to make the adjustments necessary for a truly co-ordinated system of services to unmarried mothers, the result may be that what was supposed to reduce duplication of effort, has merely added another complication to an already tangled network.

Prevention of Illegitimacy

It is difficult to talk about preventing illegitimacy because it is difficult to pinpoint its causes and to identify populations at risk. The old comfortable standby explanations about *who gets pregnant* and *why* have long outlived their usefulness. Theories about defects of mind and character previously ascribed to lower-class, poorly educated unmarried mothers, and assumptions about easy sexuality and the tolerance of illegitimacy by Negroes, do not tell us why out-of-wedlock pregnancies are occurring increasingly among white, middle-class girls and women, many of whom are well educated and come from families that have traditionally been considered pillars of society. Hypotheses about unresolved psychological conflicts do not explain the nonmarital pregnancies of those who showed no prior psychological aberrations, much less an inclination toward out-of-wedlock parenthood.

The causes of illegitimacy are complex and involve personal, social, and cultural influences that vary in their impact on the individual. Often these influences are part of a pregnancy-prone syndrome that is produced when they combine with the exigencies of the moment: sexual excitation, favorable circumstances (or unfavorable, depending upon how one looks at it), and a viable level of fertility. Many unhappy victims see this convergence of influences as "sheer dumb luck." It would be impractical to try to find individuals at their moments of vulnerability in the hope of heading off a potential pregnancy.

The most effective methods for reducing births out of wedlock in a democratic society that is permissive about sex, as ours is, are through the use of contraceptives and, in cases of conception, through abortion. Recognizing this, more and more states have been liberalizing or doing away with laws pertaining to the dissemination of birth control services and abortion. It is also being recognized increasingly that the problem of reducing the incidence of children born out of wedlock is part of the larger problem of unwanted children. It seems only a matter of time until moral outrage, cries of racial genocide, and other objections must give way to concern about the personal and social hazards involved when there are large numbers of unwanted children. As access to birth control and abortion becomes more widespread, it is to be hoped that appropriate information and services will be available so that any woman (or man, for that matter), married or unmarried, can decide on the basis of her own circumstances whether she will bear a child, regardless of her race, her place of residence, or her ability to pay.[13]

No doubt out-of-wedlock pregnancies could be reduced if people at risk could be persuaded to postpone their sexual activities until marriage. In this connection, the community is particularly concerned about adolescents. It is sometimes suggested that more young people would probably be able to keep their sexual impulses in check if, through education for family living and sex education, they could cultivate wholesome attitudes toward their own sexuality and could comprehend the place of sex in healthy family life. In themselves these are worthy goals.

Trying to reduce illegitimacy by decreasing nonmarital coitus, however, means bucking some rather formidable competition. It means counteracting a social climate that fosters the pursuit of pleasure and that is reinforced by provocative advertising aimed at exploiting a teen-age market. It means compensating for diminished family stability and for the decline in the influence of social institutions on individual behavior. It means offsetting the effects of sexually charged entertainment coupled with increased opportunity for unsupervised sexual associations. It means convincing young people that sex without marriage is all right for some people but not for others, in an age when the out-of-wedlock pregnancies of entertainment personalities receive generous press coverage, and a tri-state chain of supermarkets contracts for maternity benefits for its unmarried employees with the blessing of the local trade unions.[14]

It means also convincing people that our professed values about human worth are our true values and that sex without marriage is more demeaning to human worth than are poverty, racial discrimination, and slaughter on the battlefield. In searching for ways to reduce illegitimacy, we find more and more that our questions must extend to all phases of our living and that they apply to other countries besides our own. To talk meaningfully about preventing illegitimacy,

One would have to discuss our economy, including the consequences of poverty for the poor and the consequences of affluence for the rest of us. One would also have to discuss the values we talk about and the values we live by, the discrepancies between them, and the impact on youth of these discrepancies. One would have to discuss the effects of social and economic discrimination on Negro men, women, and children, and families. One would have to discuss the effects of affluence, our current life tempo, and the status-success-money-popularity complex on all our young people.[15]

One would also have to talk about what it must feel like to belong to a generation that has grown up in the shadow of the mushroom cloud, in a world that in one's own lifetime has never been without the threat of annihilation by a thermonuclear holocaust.

In the face of these discouraging social and world conditions, providing services for unmarried mothers may seem like palliatives that divert from the broad problems that threaten the welfare of everybody. The paths people choose as citizens to effect social change are a matter of individual conviction. Whereas, for helping people, the professional tasks remain. As long as there are unmarried mothers who need help, it is the community's responsibility to see that they receive it without having to bargain and without having to commit themselves to terms that may have little bearing on the hazards they and their babies face. If unmarried mothers can receive help promptly and unconditionally, perhaps there will be fewer for whom having an out-of-wedlock child constitutes a step toward disaster and more who will emerge from their experience with a sense of growth and with hope for the future.

NOTES

1. Vera Shlakman, "Mothers-at-Risk—Social Policy and Provision: Issues and Opportunities," in *Mothers-at-Risk,* ed. Florence Haselkorn (Garden City, N.Y.: Adelphi University School of Social Work, 1966), pp. 62–63.

2. John R. Seeley, "The Americanization of the Unconscious," *Atlantic Monthly* 208 (July 1961), pp. 68–72.

3. Jerome D. Pauker, "Girls Pregnant Out of Wedlock: Are They Pregnant Because They Are Different or Are They Different Because They Are Pregnant?" in *The Double Jeopardy, The Triple Crisis—Illegitimacy Today* (New York: National Council on Illegitimacy, 1969), p. 63.

4. U.S. Department of Health, Education, and Welfare, *Social Services for Unmarried Mothers and Their Children Provided Through Public and Voluntary Child Welfare Agencies,* prepared for the Children's Bureau by Hannah M. Adams (Washington, D.C., Government Printing Office, 1962). See also Rose Bernstein, "Gaps in Services to Unmarried Mothers," *Children* 14 (March-April 1963), pp. 49–54; and Elizabeth Herzog, "Unmarried Mothers—The Service Gap Revisited," *Children* (May-June 1967), pp. 105–10.

5. Rose Bernstein, "One Hundred Unmarried Mothers and Their Problems," unpublished study (Boston: Crittenton Hastings Home, 1961–63) p. 19.

6. Elizabeth Herzog and Rose Bernstein, "Why So Few Negro Adoptions?" *Children* 12 (January-February 1965), pp. 14–18.

7. Donald J. Bogue, *The Rural South Experiment,* Report No. 1 (Chicago: Community and Family Study Center, University of Chicago 1966).

8. Beatrice L. Garrett, "Meeting the Crisis in Foster Family Care," *Children* 13 (January-February 1966), pp. 2–8.

9. Ruth R. Middleman, "A Fuller Life for the Unmarried Mother in Residence," *Child Welfare* 45 (June 1966), pp. 349–53, and "Social Group Work in a Maternity Home," *Child Welfare* 38 (February 1959), pp. 13–18.

10. Helen B. Montgomery, "Differential Utilization of Social Work Personnel," *Children* 11 (May-June 1964), pp. 103–7.

11. "The Changing Role of Maternity Homes," *NCI* [National Council on Illegitimacy] *Newsletter* 8 (Fall 1968), pp. 5–6.

12. For reports of stages of this program, see Hester B. Curtis and Alberta deRongé, "Medical and Social Care for Unmarried Mothers," *Children* 4 (September-October 1957), pp. 174–180; and Alberta deRongé, "Services to Unmarried Mothers and Their Babies—The Role of a State Health Department," Connecticut Health Bulletin 73 (July 1959), pp. 191–96.

13. See Sidney Furie, "Birth Control and the Lower-Class Unmarried Mother," *Social Work* 11 (January 1966), pp. 42–49; and Naomi Thomas Gray, "Family Planning and Social Welfare's Responsibility," *Social Casework* 48 (October 1966), pp. 487–93.

14. Miami *Herald,* January 22, 1970.

15. Herzog, "Unmarried Mothers," p. 110.